FISCAL THEORY AND POLITICAL ECONOMY

SELECTED ESSAYS

By

JAMES M. BUCHANAN

Chapel Hill

THE UNIVERSITY OF NORTH CAROLINA PRESS

Manufactured in the United States of America

PRINTED BY THE SEEMAN PRINTERY, DURHAM, N. C.

2ND PRINTING
NORTH CAROLINA STATE UNIVERSITY PRINT SHOP, RALEIGH, N. C.

Dedicated to the memory
of my Mother

LILA SCOTT BUCHANAN

ACKNOWLEDGMENTS

SIX of the essays included here have been previously published. I gratefully acknowledge the permission of the editors of *The Journal of Political Economy, The American Economic Review, The Journal of Law and Economics,* and *Studi economici* to allow me to reprint the relevant essays included in this volume.

All of the essays were completed and the collection was initially submitted for publication prior to to the appearance of Professor Richard A. Musgrave's treatise, *The Theory of Public Finance.* This important work includes material that is relevant to many of the points discussed in the separate essays. For this reason, an explicit explanation of failure to make reference to this book seems appropriate.

I am indebted to the Old Dominion Foundation and to the Gee Institute for Research in the Social Sciences of the University of Virginia for their aid in the publication of this work.

JAMES M. BUCHANAN

Charlottesville, Virginia
February, 1960

CONTENTS

Introduction 3

I. The Pure Theory of Government Finance: A Suggested Approach 8

II. "La scienza delle finanze": The Italian Tradition in Fiscal Theory 24

III. Social Choice, Democracy, and Free Markets 75

IV. Individual Choice in Voting and the Market 90

V. Positive Economics, Welfare Economics, and Political Economy 105

VI. The Methodology of Incidence Theory: A Critical Review of Some Recent Contributions 125

VII. Comparative Tax Analysis and Economic Methodology 151

VIII. Federalism and Fiscal Equity 170

Index of Authors 191

Index of Subjects 193

FISCAL THEORY AND POLITICAL ECONOMY

INTRODUCTION

SO long as the Cold War continues, the proportion of national output utilized by government seems unlikely to be reduced sizeably. As society attempts to adjust its institutions, and as its members try to adjust their thinking, to a relatively permanent requirement that approximately one-fourth of all production be devoted to the satisfaction of "public" rather than private needs, the absence of an acceptable theory of the public or collective economy becomes acutely evident. Scholars can hardly continue to discuss the organizing principles of the private economy in abstraction from the public sector. And they do little by way of improvement when they merely incorporate the appropriate governmental variables as exogenous to their models of economic activity. Governmental decisions are no more exogenous than are those made in the private economy. Collective decisions arise out of the behavior of individuals responding to alternatives placed before them. Any approach to a complete or satisfactory treatment of the public economy must examine as a central feature the way in which collective decisions are made.

The foundations upon which an acceptable modern fiscal theory can be built are only in the process of discovery and exploration. This important sub-discipline on the borderline between economics and politics has only recently begun to attract the attention of scholars. The task of formal construction remains largely undone. The first stage is one of criticism; the shortcomings of the traditional works in public finance must be isolated and identified. The essays in this book represent various efforts, made over a ten-year period, to note some of the limitations in orthodox thinking on fiscal theory, to raise what appear to be some of the relevant questions, and to explore some of the challenging issues that arise in this field of study. The volume is properly interpreted as a progress report, a balance sheet struck after a decade's academic accounting period.

As its title suggests, the first essay was written as an exploratory approach toward filling an obvious gap in the English-language literature in fiscal theory. Almost without exception, scholars have failed to make explicit their assumptions concerning the form of the polity. This may not have been a serious omission when political decisions were quantitatively unimportant in their impact on the private economy, but it becomes a glaring fault of fiscal theory in the mid-twentieth century. In this first essay, two opposing theories of the state are shown to lead to two separate theories of the public economy. More complete examination would allow several sub-categories within each of these to be isolated, but the broad dichotomy is sufficient to point up the issue. As will be clear to the reader, I consider the "individualistic" assumptions to be the only appropriate ones for democratically-organized societies, and much of the discussion to be found in the subsequent essays is based on this conviction. Knut Wicksell's charge that much of the discussion in fiscal theory proceeds on the implicit and unrecognized assumption that the society is ruled by a benevolent despot remains almost as true today as it was sixty years ago.

The initial essay was completed before I became familiar with the Italian tradition in fiscal theory. Cursory examination of this literature revealed that the Italian scholars have devoted much more careful attention to the relationships between political conceptions and fiscal norms. After the original publication of this essay, I was fortunate to get the opportunity for a year's research on the Italian fiscal tradition. Critical discussion of a whole doctrinal tradition can best be appreciated when the critic's own frame of reference is understood. For this reason, I have included the results of my research on the Italian fiscal theory, originally intended as a separate monograph, as the second, and longest, essay in this volume.

The third and fourth selections were jointly written. The argument of these essays follows directly from the approach to fiscal theory suggested in the first essay. I attempt here to examine the process of collective choice under the individualistic assumptions about the state. The casual reader, accustomed to thinking in terms of artificially constructed and mutually exclusive sub-categories in the social sciences, may question why the third essay, written as a general critique of Kenneth Arrow's *Social Choice and Individual Values,* is included in a volume devoted to fiscal theory. Such questions as this vanish, however, when the central role of collective decision-making in fiscal theory is appreciated. Only the work in welfare economics, which provided the background and motivation for Arrow's provocative effort, has adequately recognized the need for a bridge between individual decisions and collective decisions. The fourth essay, arising directly from the discussion of the third, specifically compares individual behavior in collective decision-making with individual behavior in making private economic choices.

The fifth selection is devoted to an examination of the role of the economist in developing propositions for collective action. I have tried here to locate the economist *qua* economist in the whole collective decision-making complex. Drawing heavily on Knut Wicksell's major contribution to fiscal theory, an appropriate role for the "positive" political economist is outlined, a role that does not involve the deliberate introduction of individual ethical judgments. The impact of the conclusions of this essay upon the possibility of developing fiscal norms remains to be developed in projected works.

The first five essays, with the exception of portions of the second, are, broadly speaking, devoted to the development of a single general theme. Fiscal theory rests on both economic theory and political theory, and the bridge between these two disciplines must be provided in any examination of collective choice. The conception of the collectivity affects in important ways the appropriateness of the fiscal propositions advanced. In an individualistic society, collective choice must represent some composite of individual choices, and a fiscal theory that fails to incorporate this fact is likely to lead to unintended results.

The three final essays in the volume are somewhat more positivistic. They are fundamentally methodological. Here it is argued that fiscal propositions are unlikely to lead to correct predictions unless relevant alternatives are subjected to comparison. The right questions must be raised before the correct answers can be expected. Essentially my efforts here represent a plea for fiscal theorists to shake off Marshallian partial equilibrium methods in application to general equilibrium problems. In more particular terms, the sixth essay is a critical review of the recent, and continuing, debate over the incidence of excise taxes. The seventh selection covers developments in the "excess burden" controversy, and it explicitly attempts to extend the conclusions more generally by an application of the appropriate methodological principles. The final essay, although not specifically methodological in nature, employs the general equilibrium approach to arrive at a solution to a specific problem, the fiscal problem of federal political structures.

The incorporation of general equilibrium methods in fiscal theory does not require that the analyst employ Walrasian models. But care must be taken to treat dependent variables as if they are dependent; the failure to do this has led to misleading conclusions in many cases. In its simplest form, this error amounts to a failure to recognize the fundamental two-sidedness of the government's fiscal account. Correct analysis must normally be conducted in differential terms; changes in one variable can be examined only on the assumption that compensating or offsetting changes occur elsewhere in the system. My emphasis on the importance of this methodological issue will explain my evaluation of the major Italian contribution to fiscal theory which is discussed in the second essay.

The two major themes of the volume are closely related. If government is conceived as a decision-making entity apart from private citizens, the consumption of collectively-provided services may also be considered to have little effect on the behavior of private individuals. The collective decisions are exogenous to the private economic calculus of individual families, and these decisions affect this calculus only in so far as taxes reduce the opportunities open for private or market utilization of resources. Fiscal theory becomes, therefore, the study of the adjustments in individual behavior made necessary by the imposition of taxes of various sorts. The English-language tradition in fiscal theory, still dominated by the political presuppositions of the classical economists, fits this model surprisingly well.

De Viti De Marco correctly emphasized the simple point that, in democratically-organized societies, producers and consumers of collective goods and services are identical in the sense that both are included in the decision-making group. Regardless of the redistribution that the fiscal structure may accomplish, either incidentally or intentionally, the one-man-one-vote ideal of democratic choice-making implies universal participation in decisions. Individual decisions must turn on some comparison of costs and benefits, and the neglect of the expenditure side of the account involves serious bias in the results. The assumptions made concerning the political structure significantly affect the methodological setting within which positive propositions of fiscal theory may be developed.

It must, of course, be recognized that separately written essays cannot be merged into a completely suitable organic whole. Individual pieces include sections which are relevant to the localized discussion but which diverge from the themes that associate the separate essays one with another. And whereas the treatment of a single point may have seemed essential to complete the argument of an independently-written essay, its inclusion in a collection of this sort may involve some repetition.

I

THE PURE THEORY OF GOVERNMENT FINANCE: A SUGGESTED APPROACH*

I

A FRAMEWORK for the pure theory of government finance may be erected on either of two political foundations, which represent, in turn, two separate and opposing theories of the state. Since neither construction is entirely appropriate when applied to all the problems faced in the fiscal area, the proper methodological procedure seems to be the setting-up of alternate theories.

In the first, or what may be called the "organismic," theory, the state, including all individuals within it, is conceived as a single organic entity. In the second, the state is represented as the sum of its individual members acting in a collective capacity. The individual and the state may be fundamentally opposing forces in the second concept, while in the organic view, the state, or general interest, subsumes all individual interests. The theory of government finance based upon the second concept of the state may be called the "individualistic" one.

These two approaches have not been clearly separated or distinguished in the literature of government finance.[1] Some variant of the organismic theory normally has been applied to the public-expenditure side, while the individualistic theory has been pre-

* Reprinted with slight modification by permission from the *Journal of Political Economy*. LVII (December, 1949), 496-505.

1. This paper was written before the author was familiar with Italian fiscal theory. The Italian literature is characterized by a much more careful consideration of the political presuppositions.

dominantly employed in considering the distribution of the tax load. Fiscal marginalism has been extended to define the optimum allocation of public expenditures among alternative uses, that is, in the pure theory of budgeting. The allocation of total tax burden among alternative sources, has, on the other hand, traditionally been discussed in terms of the relative tax pressures imposed upon individuals.[2] Such asymmetry, while perhaps appropriate in practical application, does not appear formally complete. It seems desirable to develop the two theories independently at the outset.

II

In the organismic theory the state is considered as a single decision-making unit acting for society as a whole. Presumably, it seeks to maximize some conceptually quantifiable magnitude. A major difficulty is apparent in the determination of what is to be maximized. What is the common denominator to which the alternative goals of the collective entity may be reduced for comparative purposes, analogous to the equally vague, but less elusive, "satisfaction" or "utility" for the individual? A common denominator is necessary as a starting point in order that any one "configuration of the economic system" may be regarded as better or worse than any other. This general end of society may be called "general welfare" or "social utility"; the name is not important.

"Social utility" is a function of many variables. The maximizing process will include the manipulation of many factors which lie outside the scope of fiscal theory. The structure of the whole social organization is itself a property subject to change. Many of the variables are non-economic; and, even among those which can be classified as economic in nature, a relatively small proportion can be embraced in fiscal theory. The non-fiscal variables, therefore, must be accepted as parameters for the smaller system, and "social utility" must be maximized, subject to the constraints imposed. The variables to be determined in the fiscal process fall

2. There have been, of course, certain elements of each approach present in most competent works. The individual benefits from public expenditures have never been entirely overlooked, nor have the social effects of taxation been completely neglected.

into two groups—the expenditure variables and the tax variables. The amounts of public expenditure allocated to each use comprise the expenditure variables. The amounts of tax imposed upon each economic entity or tax source (individuals, business units, estates, etc.) comprise the tax variables. There are as many variables in the fiscal system as there are expenditure outlets and tax sources. Any allocation of the total tax load represents a solution of the whole set of tax variables. Any distribution of public expenditure among competing uses indicates a fixing of values for all the expenditure variables. Included in the setting of these values is the determination of total tax load and total public expenditures.

It is the function of the "fiscal brain" or "computer" to select the value of these many variables which will maximize social utility. The maximizing process consists of a simultaneous determination of all the variables on both sides. The necessary condition for a maximum is produced when the partial derivatives vanish or when a dollar's tax load upon each economic entity deducts from social utility an amount equivalent to that added by a dollar's expenditure in each line.

It is important to note that the optimum values for the tax variables cannot be determined independently except for given values for the expenditure variables. The allocation of the tax load which will maximize social utility or, in this case, minimize deductions from utility, will be different for each separate distribution of total expenditure. Similarly, the distribtuion of expenditure which will maximize welfare will be a function of the tax variables. The relative additions to social utility provided by the offering of public services to particular groups will be dependent in part upon the relative tax loads imposed.

The principle of taxation which is appropriate in this theoretical framework is that of the Edgeworth-Pigou variety. The relevant criteria of comparison are reductions from social welfare or utility; the "least-aggregate-sacrifice" approach is the correct one. The principle of equimarginal "sacrifice" or, better, "subtraction," if values are given for the expenditure variables, provides an acceptable rule for the apportionment of the total tax burden. For each allocation of public expenditure the satisfaction of this principle will define an apportionment which will minimize the subtraction from social utility. It should be emphasized, however, that subtraction can be used only with reference to a social, not an individual, concept of utility.[3] For each given distribution of public expenditures the necessary condition for the optimum allocation of the tax load is reached when a dollar's tax upon each economic entity deducts an equivalent amount from aggregate social utility. The economic entities for such tax comparisons may or may not be individuals in this analysis.

Symmetrically, given values for the tax variables, an allocation of total public expenditure among alternative uses can be found which will maximize social welfare. This is also given by the application of the economic principle, or here the principle of "equimarginal addition." The necessary condition for the optimum is reached when a dollar of expenditure yields the same return, in addition to social utility, in each line. This allocation is independently determinate only for fixed values of all the tax variables. For each change in the apportionment of the tax load, a new optimum allocation of expenditure must be found.

Little more can be included in the framework of the organismic theory. Vague and general terms, such as "social utility" and "social welfare," are of little use in the discussion of policy problems. The theoretical steps in the maximizing of social utility offer little or no direct guidance to governmental fiscal authorities. As was mentioned earlier, this approach has been utilized largely in the theory of budgeting. Here it can provide a primary frame of reference, within which issues may be discussed, policies formulated, and decisions reached. Even in this limited usage, however, the functional interdependence of the whole fiscal system must not be overlooked.

III

The focus is completely shifted in the individualistic theory. The individual replaces the state as the basic structural unit. The

3. In this sense the principle of equimarginal sacrifice implies nothing about the ultimate equalization of incomes as a result of its application. This implication arises only when individuals are considered as the basic fiscal entities and when some assumption is made about the identities of individuals as pleasure machines.

state has its origin in, and depends for its continuance upon, the desires of individuals to fulfill a certain portion of their wants collectively. The state has no ends other than those of its individual members and is not a separate decision-making unit. State decisions are, in the final analysis, the collective decisions of individuals.

The income of the state represents payment made by individuals out of their economic resources in exchange for services provided. In the provision of these services the state is, in most cases, in a perfectly monopolistic position. However, it does not seek to maximize net revenue. Services are offered at cost. The supply curve of public services is an average-cost curve, not a marginal-cost curve. This applies, of course, only to the aggregate of all public services considered in the abstract as some sort of homogeneous magnitude. In no way does it imply that each particular service is "sold" to individuals at the average cost of provision. In the social-service state many are offered free; others at marginal-cost prices. In very few cases (the particular services provided in return for fees being the major exception) is there much connection between payments made to government by individuals and the special benefits enjoyed. But, when the aggregate of all public services is considered, the attempt is made to cover total cost. In effect, if public services are categorized, the "losses" to the government resulting from the provision of some must be balanced by "profits" accruing from the provision of others.

The extent and range of public services are determined by the collective willingness of individuals to purchase them. Services will be extended as long as the marginal aggregate benefits are held to exceed the marginal costs. Ideally, the fiscal process represents a *quid pro quo* transaction between the government and all individuals collectively considered.[4] The benefit principle must be applicable in this sense.[5]

4. The "pure" theory should be formulated on the assumption of stability in the economic system and thus balance between the two sides of the fiscal account. "Functional" finance precepts can be fitted into the framework at a second theoretical level.

5. The meaning of "benefit principle" and *quid pro quo* as employed in this essay should be clarified. A *quid pro quo* relationship exists when the individual pays to government an amount in taxes equivalent in value to him of *the amount*

Each individual is subjected to some fiscal pressure; his economic resources are reduced by the amount of tax that he bears. His real income is increased by the benefits that he receives from government services. The allocation of total tax load among individuals must be combined with the distribution of benefits from publicly provided services in any complete theoretical framework. However, in this approach the imputation of specific benefits to individuals has been almost entirely glossed over in the orthodox literature. Overwhelming attention has been devoted to the allocation of the tax burden.

The practical omission of the benefit side can be attributed in part to the erroneous foundations of the benefit theory of taxation. In the legitimate rejection of the benefit principle as the universal norm for the distribution of the tax burden, too much was thrown out. This principle, widely accepted in the seventeenth and eighteenth centuries[6] and reintroduced in a more sophisticated form in the 1880's,[7] is based upon the premise that there should exist a *quid pro quo* fiscal relationship between the individual and government. The principle has been overthrown for two basic reasons. First, there appears no precise manner of imputing shares of the aggregate common benefit from public services to specific individuals. A significant portion of public funds is expended for the "general welfare," not to benefit particular persons or groups. Second, it is recognized that the underlying *quid pro quo* ideal is not at all acceptable in the modern state.[8]

---

of public services which he receives. In other words, a *market-type* relationship exists between the individual and the government. The *quid pro quo* principle does not imply that, if an all-or-none decision, or a discriminatory decision were to be imposed, the individual would be as well off without government as with it. The validity of introducing this all-or-none comparison involves the appropriateness or inappropriateness of using Marshallian consumers' surplus in evaluating government services. Much confusion is present in the literature of the benefit theory on this point; the two possible meanings of "benefit" theory have not been clearly distinguished. This confusion has, in turn, led to much erroneous discussion of real-world policy issues.

6. For an excellent short history of the early benefit theories see Erik Lindahl, *Die Gerechtigkeit der Besteuerung* (Lund: Gleerupska Universitets-Bokhandeln, 1919), pp. 118 ff.

7. In the works of Pantaleoni, Sax, and De Viti De Marco.

8. Wagner clearly pointed out that, once the government began to provide social services, the benefit theory became completely inapplicable (Adolph Wagner, *Finanzwissenschaft* [Leipzig: C. F. Winter, 1890], II, 431-42).

But these two basic objections to the benefit principle are of fundamentally different natures. The first is a technical or an administrative difficulty, which prevents the principle from having direct applicability to policy. The second rests upon a rejection of the ethical premise that there should be an individual *quid pro quo*. If we accept the *quid pro quo* ideal, the benefit principle is correct in the abstract; and the problem of individual imputation of benefits is a technical, not a theoretical, problem. De Viti De Marco recognized this and therefore accepted as a working hypothesis the return of benefits roughly in proportion to incomes. Thus, adopting the ethical standard of the benefit principle, he justified a system of proportional taxation. In such a theoretical framework the apportionment of the tax load is directly dependent upon the benefit hypothesis formulated. If benefits were assumed to accrue equally per head, De Viti De Marco would have held a system of poll taxation to be appropriate.[9]

The rejection of the benefit theory of taxation should rest not upon the difficulty of individual isolation of specific benefits but upon the unacceptability of the ethical ideal of the individual *quid pro quo*. Once this commutative fiscal relationship of the individual with government is thrown out as the norm, is there any value to be gained from attempts at surmounting the technical problem of individual-benefit imputation? In orthodox fiscal theory the implied answer to this question has been "No," with the result that benefit considerations have been seriously neglected. The whole expenditure side of the fiscal account has been given little attention. In the individualistic approach, both the total amount of public expenditure and its allocation among uses have been assumed to be fixed outside the pale of fiscal theory.

Fiscal analysis has proceeded as if all taxes were net subtractions from social income, never to be returned. J. B. Say's dictum that "the value paid to government by the taxpayer is given with-

9. Thus Graham says: "Since the value of most governmental services to the individual members of a community cannot be accurately assessed, nor can one take or leave them as he will, it could with some reason be contended that the ideal principle of allocation of the burden of taxation is neither progression nor proportionality but uniformity, that is, that all members of the community should pay the same amount" (Frank D. Graham, *Social Goals and Economic Institutions* [Princeton: Princeton University Press, 1942], p. 234).

out equivalent or return"[10] has been implicitly accepted, although lip service has been paid to its inherent fallacy. It is evident that such a limitation leaves the body of theory incomplete and inadequate. If benefits from public services accrue to individuals as a group (and this is impossible to deny), it follows that specific benefits are received by particular individuals regardless of the technical difficulty of dividing the common benefit among them. Aggregate benefits must be in the nature of a quantitative magnitude and thus subject to conceptual divisibility. Benefits simply cannot be forgotten. Wicksell very clearly pointed out that the procedure of leaving out the benefit side amounts to concluding that each individual actually gets no benefit whatsoever from the government services provided him.[11] And, since the addition of any number of zeroes yields a zero result, the aggregate benefit must also be zero if such an omissive assumption is made.[12] On this basis no public expenditure is theoretically justified. Furthermore, if no individuals in the social unit receive any benefit, it is apparent that no funds will be granted for the support of government. No tax bills could ever be passed by an elected representative assembly.

Only if individual shares of the aggregate benefit from public services are held to be roughly equal can the concentration of analysis on the allocation of tax burden alone be theoretically justified. It seems likely that this is the assumption made by some writers.[13] If phrases such as "chargeable against the whole com-

10. *A Treatise on Political Economy,* trans. C. R. Prinsep (Philadelphia: J. B. Lippincott & Co., 1855), p. 413.

11. Knut Wicksell, *Finanztheoretische Untersuchungen* (Jena: Gustav Fischer, 1896), p. 82.

12. *Ibid.*: "Ist jener Nutzen für die einzelnen Mitglieder der Gesamtheit gleich Null, so wird auch der Gesamtnutzen nicht von Null verschieden sein können."

13. For example, compare the following statements by J. S. Mill and Bastable:

"If a person or class of persons receives so small a share of the benefit as makes it necessary to raise the question, there is something else than taxation which is amiss, and the thing to be done is to remedy the defect, instead of recognizing it and making it a ground for demanding less taxes" (J. S. Mill, *Principles of Political Economy* [Boston: C. Little & James Brown, 1848], II, 345).

"But from the difficulty of discrimination it seems better to adhere to the

munity"[14] and "throughout the population"[15] can be interpreted as containing the implication that the benefits from most public services are shared equally among all citizens, then the approach has been internally consistent. If individual shares in the common benefit are considered equivalent, the real problems in fiscal theory are limited to the tax side, since equals would cancel equals when benefits are included in comparing the fiscal positions of individuals.

This necessary condition for the practical omission of benefit considerations should be clearly stated and its applicability empirically tested in so far as is possible. The dependence of the validity of the orthodox approach upon this rather narrow assumption was recognized by Kaizl and by De Viti De Marco.[16] But a general theoretical framework should not be so limited, even if this condition is made explicit.

The difficult problem of individual-benefit imputation must be squarely faced. It is impossible to speak of the "burden of taxation" without considering, at the same time, the benefits from expenditure made out of such taxation.[17] Even the setting-up of untested explicit hypotheses concerning benefit accrual is preferable to omission altogether.[18] The most realistic hypothesis might well

---

general rule of distributing taxation without direct reference to the results of expenditure on different classes. Injustices of this kind ought to be corrected not by the redistribution of taxation but by alterations of outlay" (C. F. Bastable, *Public Finance,* 2nd ed. [London: Macmillan & Co., 1895], p. 312).

14. Henry C. Simons, *Personal Income Taxation* (Chicago: University of Chicago Press, 1938), p. 31.

15. E. D. Allen and O. H. Brownlee, *Economics of Public Finance* (New York: Prentice-Hall, 1947), p. 192.

16. ". . . das fundamentale Corollar der heutigen Auffassung der Steuergerechtigkeit . . . dass nicht nur die Last der Steuer gerecht vertheilt werde, sondern dass auch die Vortheile und Emolumente der öffentlichen Institutionen gleich vertheilt werden, dass sie Allen gleich zugänglich seien" (Kaizl, *Finanzwissenschaft,* II, 200, cited by Lindahl, *op. cit.,* p. 133).

"Thus one may abstract from the service of providing public security, if one assumes, and if the assumption corresponds to the facts, that the amount of security provided is equal for all productive enterprises that exchange their products. Thus, it is as if one were to cancel a common term in two terms of an equation" (Antonio De Viti De Marco, *First Principles of Public Finance,* tr. E. P. Marget [London: Jonathan Cape, 1936], p. 52).

17. Tibor Barna, *Redistribution of Income through Public Finance in 1937* (London: Oxford University Press, 1945), p. 3.

18. *Ibid.*

be that of equal per head sharing,[19] but alternative ones should be considered and tested if possible.

The final economic position of the individual, after his relationship with the "fisc," can be expressed in the form of a balance between the two sides of the fiscal account. (If we accept the *quid pro quo* premise, this balance will always be zero.)[20] This balance can be called the "fiscal residuum."[21] If an individual's tax burden exceeds the value of benefits received from government services, he will have a positive residuum. He will pay a net tax. If the value of the share of public benefits which he enjoys exceeds the value of the contributions which he makes to government, the residuum will be negative. The individual will receive a net benefit. Only by a comparison of the residuums of individuals can the total effects of a fiscal system be analyzed and evaluated. Tax-burden comparisons alone are likely to yield quite different and perhaps misleading conclusions.[22]

19. The use of this hypothesis has been found to yield important results in some areas. I have applied this to the theory of inter-governmental fiscal adjustment in a federal state and have been able to work out a determinate system of transfers without reference to particular tax burdens or particular service standards.

For another example of application to a similar problem see J. R. and U. K. Hicks, *Standards of Local Expenditure* (London: Cambridge University Press, 1943), p. 3.

20. In calculating the residuum discussed here, the existence of a positive value will indicate only that, if he could choose freely, the individual would choose *less* public services, not that he would choose to eliminate government altogether if given an all-or-none choice. It seems clear that if the latter decision were to be imposed, the benefit principle of taxation would be satisfied with almost any possible distribution of the tax load, that is, each individual would have a negative residuum calculated in this way (see *supra,* footnote 5).

The existence of a zero residuum, as defined in this essay, means that the "market" value of services received is equal to taxes paid. The meaning is precisely analogous to that implied by the statement that, in ordinary market behavior, the individual "gets what he pays for." The distinction between the *quid pro quo* and "mutual gains from trade" in considerations of ordinary markets is that between exchange made at the margin and exchange made on all-or-none bases.

21. The concept of a fiscal balance or residuum was utilized by Wicksell in a different sense (*op. cit.,* p. 81).

22. The comparative study of the burdens of state and local taxes in New York and Illinois for 1936, published by the Twentieth Century Fund in *Studies in Current Tax Problems* (New York, 1937), can be used as an example. On the basis of the tax-load comparisons alone, the tax load was found to be heavier in New York than in Illinois on eight out of the ten hypothetical families studied (p. 34).

By making the assumption of benefit accrual equally per head, and including

This approach enables a general classification of fiscal systems to be made, comprising three major groups. First, those systems which tend to increase the inequality in the distribution of real income among individuals can be classified as "aggravative." This type of system would be indicated if low-income individuals showed positive residuums, i.e., taxes in excess of benefits, while the high-income receivers showed negative residuums. Some systems of the sixteenth and seventeenth centuries which collected revenues from large elements of the population in the main for the support of the royal household and the nobility would perhaps be characteristic.

Second, those fiscal systems which tend to return to all individuals approximately the equivalent of their contributions and thus to have no net effect on the prevailing distribution of real income can be classified as "status quo" systems.[23] This type would be indicated if a calculation of the fiscal residuums for individuals in all income brackets yielded roughly zero results. This type is perhaps best represented in the fiscal systems of the early nineteenth century, when a large share of revenue was collected from levies on property and a major portion was expended in the provision of protection, internal and external.

Third, those fiscal systems which tend to redress the prevailing distribution of real income toward more equality can be classified as "equalitarian" or "redistributive." If people in the low-income groups receive more in benefits than they pay in taxes and the upper-income groups contribute more than they receive in benefits,

New York and Illinois state and local expenditures in addition to the computed tax-load figures, it was found that the results were significantly changed. Where only two New York families out of ten were found to be in advantageous positions when tax burdens alone were considered, seven New York families became favored in fiscal treatment when the benefit side was included.

23. As in the preceding footnotes 5 and 20, it will be useful to clarify the analysis at this point. By saying that the fiscal system characterized by zero residuums would not redistribute real income, I am using real income in an objectively measurable sense. In so far as the "total" benefits from government exceed the "total" costs by a greater amount for some individuals than for others, a net redistribution of psychic income is accomplished, even in a "status quo" fiscal system. Psychic income is redistributed by the fiscal system here in the same manner in which it is redistributed by market exchange. It seems useful to ignore this subjectively-determined concept here, and to define real income in terms of "market" values.

this type of system is indicated. This is, of course, the type which is characteristic of the modern state. A large share of revenue is derived from the proceeds of progressive income taxes, and a major portion of expenditures in peacetime is devoted to the provision of social services.

As was stated earlier, regardless of the kind of fiscal system, there should exist the *quid pro quo* relationship between government and all individuals taken together. This is represented by a balancing of the net taxes paid by certain individuals against the net benefits received by others in the first and third classifications. Only in the second type of system does the collective equalization of benefits and taxes imply that each individual receives in benefits the approximate equivalent of contribution made.

This simple classification represents nothing new.[24] It seems essential, however, that it be employed as the primary frame of reference within which more specific problems may be placed. One should bear in mind that the classification refers to fiscal systems, not to tax systems. Tax systems have been traditionally classified as regressive, proportional, and progressive, based upon the ratio of tax burden to income at different income levels. These terms are useful in describing the nature of a tax system, but they do not describe the fiscal system, as would appear to be the case in ordinary usage.

Progressive taxation has been justified because it leads to a more equal distribution of income among individuals. Standing alone, the statement that progressive taxation does redistribute real income is not true. It can be true only on the basis of certain assumptions about the other half of the fiscal system. If individual shares in the common benefit from public expenditures are all equal or approximately so, then progressive taxation will lead to a more equal distribution. But so will proportional taxation on the same basis.[25] Without considering the imputation of individual benefits, all that may be stated categorically is that progressive taxa-

24. Cf. W. J. Shultz and C. L. Harriss, *American Public Finance,* 5th ed. (New York: Prentice-Hall, 1949), p. 104.

25. The statement that progressive taxation will redistribute incomes but that proportional taxation will not, implies that benefits are returned to individuals in proportion to incomes and wealth.

tion will produce a more equal distribution of income than would proportional or regressive taxation. One cannot say that it will produce a redistribution; it may or may not.[26]

If a major share of governmental expenditures were allocated to provide protection to the property rights of the wealthy classes, then even a progressive tax system might not prevent the fiscal system from increasing real income inequality. On the other hand, if benefits were wholly in the nature of social services, poor relief, unemployment compensation, etc., then a *regressive* tax system might well be a part of a *redistributive* fiscal system.[27] Conversely, public expenditures made for the benefit of low-income groups may be financed by taxes on those same or even lower-income groups.[28] Certainly, if a significant tax increase or change in the structure of the tax system of any kind is proposed, the ultimate manner in which the proceeds are to be expended should, in part, determine the nature of the change. The same amount of redistribution may be as well accomplished by the levy of a sales tax to provide expanded social services as by an increase in the higher-bracket income-tax rates to finance additional defense expenditure. Since redistribution is only one goal of responsible social policy in the modern state, fiscal policy should reflect such possible alternatives.

The ratio of tax burden to income at various income levels should be separated from any underlying ideas concerning final distributive effects. Owing to the connotation which has caused

26. The emphasis upon the redistribution effects of the tax side alone is indicated in the following quotation from the *Annual Economic Report* submitted to the President by the Council of Economic Advisers in January, 1949: "The federal personal income tax has reduced somewhat the concentration of income. In 1947, for example, the lowest three-fifths of families received 29 per cent of total money income before tax compared to 31 per cent after tax, while the share of the upper one-fifth was reduced by taxes from 48 to 46" (reprinted in *United States News and World Report,* January 14, 1949, p. 72).

See also R. A. Musgrave and Tun Thin, "Income Tax Progression, 1929-48," *Journal of Political Economy,* LVI (1948), 498-514.

27. In 1947 a state-wide general sales tax was imposed in Tennessee, with most of the proceeds earmarked for expenditure in the provision of educational services. It can plausibly be argued that the collection of the tax and the expenditure of the proceeds taken together are redistributive.

28. The British case seems applicable here. Should not the "redistributive" effects of the food subsidies be carefully scrutinized, considering the enormous levies on tobacco and liquor?

them to be so sharply categorized with such distributive implications, perhaps it would be better if the terms "regression," "proportion," and "progression" were discarded.

The theoretical framework in the individualistic approach does not include the specification of a single fiscal system to be adopted by the society. The ends to be served by the fiscal system are determined by political decisions. The framework does, however, enable the fiscal specialist to indicate the alternate distributions of tax burdens and public expenditures which will yield the desired results. If, for example, the society desires a fiscal system which will not affect the prevailing distribution of real incomes, any number of fiscal structures, tax-burden and expenditure allocations can be formulated which will approximate it. Further, if this status quo ideal, plus an allocation of public expenditures, is given, the single most appropriate tax structure can be outlined.

A similar approach is suggested for other than status quo norms. The redress of the prevailing income distribution toward greater equality has been accepted as one of the fundamental purposes of the fiscal system in the modern state. The fiscal scientist can provide policy-makers with practical guides to action in several ways. If the desired degree of redistribution is known, the alternate pairs of tax-burden and public-expenditure allocations which will yield this result can be indicated. If this, plus the existing public expenditure pattern, is known, it is possible to set up the tax system, assuming in this case that attainment is possible under the given conditions. On the other side, given the degree of redistribution and the apportionment of the tax load, the expenditure pattern can be established.

Society, however, does not normally make concrete decisions concerning the amount of redistribution desired. Rather, it determines an allocation of expenditures among uses and a distribution of the tax load which will, when combined, cause the fiscal system to be redistributive. The role of the fiscal scientist *qua* scientist in this situation is clear. With these properties he can determine roughly the amount of redistribution of real incomes actually accomplished through the fiscal process.[29] He is then

29. This is the approach taken in the path-breaking work of Barna (*op. cit.*).

able to indicate alternative tax and expenditure allocations which would yield approximately equivalent redistribution results, some of which might result in significantly different effects upon the economy. It is perhaps in the area of estimating the amount of redistribution carried out by the fiscal system that the most productive empirical work in the whole field of government finance can now be carried on. The traditional difficulty encountered in the attempt to impute specific shares of the benefits from public services to individuals, even upon the recognition of the communal nature of the aggregate benefit, should not be deterrent. It will not be, once it is fully comprehended that the benefit side cannot be left out and any sort of generalized theoretical framework set up. It must be recognized that the omission yields results equivalent to those produced by adopting even more arbitrary assumptions than the heroic ones admittedly required concerning the incidence of public expenditures. With the expansion of government activity toward the provision of social services, and services to particular economic or social groups, the problem should present less of a dilemma. For example, the individual benefits from farm price supports can be more readily estimated than those from defense expenditures.

IV

In both the organismic and the individualistic aproaches to fiscal theory, the paramount need is that the interdependence of the two sides of the fiscal process be clearly understood. Both approaches require parallel consideration to be given to the determination of the expenditure allocation and the apportionment of tax burden. In neither theory can either side be analyzed in isolation.

The organismic framework gives a much more complete normative behavior pattern for the fiscal authority. Since the government is the basic entity, the fiscal theory reduces to a statement of an applied maximization problem. The major obstacles lie in the attempts at translation of the theoretical guides to action into a realistic approach to practical policy. It becomes extremely arduous, if not impossible, to fill in the theoretical framework with empirical content.

In the individualistic approach the government represents only the collective will of individuals and cannot be considered the originator of action in an abstract sense. The fisc cannot be assumed to maximize anything. The fiscal system exists as one channel through which certain collective desires may be accomplished. The content of theory becomes the setting-up of a structural framework to enable the results of policies to be evaluated.

II

"LA SCIENZA DELLE FINANZE": THE ITALIAN TRADITION IN FISCAL THEORY*

I. INTRODUCTION

NOW that the important early Swedish contributions on monetary and cycle theory have been made available, it may be asserted that the single most important national body of doctrine which remains largely unknown to and unappreciated by English-language economists is the Italian work in fiscal theory. The linguistic barrier has served effectively to prevent the dissemination of the Italian contribution in this area of applied economics, an area which has been an Italian speciality for at least a century. The only book which has been translated is De Viti De Marco, *First Principles of Public Finance*.[1] While this book is perhaps the

* Much of the research upon which this paper is based was conducted while the author held a Fulbright research scholarship in Italy. I am especially indebted to Professors Giannino Parravicini and Sergio Steve for their assistance in facilitating this research as well as for their helpful comments on earlier versions of this paper. I also gratefully acknowledge the helpful suggestions made by Professors Luigi Einaudi and Gustavo Del Vecchio, both of whom read earlier versions of this paper. Their intimate acquaintance with the whole body of doctrine discussed here has made these suggestions especially valuable. Errors of fact, interpretation, and analysis remain, of course, entirely my own.

1. Antonio De Viti De Marco, *First Principles of Public Finance*, tr. E. P. Marget (London: Jonathan Cape, 1936).

A few additional essays have recently been translated and are included in *Classics in the Theory of Public Finance*, ed. by R. A. Musgrave and A. T. Peacock (London: Macmillan, 1958). Essays by Pantaleoni, Barone, Montemartini, and Mazzola are included.

most outstanding single work, its contribution cannot readily be appreciated by those not familiar with the Italian tradition. This explains the extremely divergent reactions of Henry Simons and F. C. Benham to the book, Simons calling it a "monument to confusion," while Benham was acclaiming it as the best book ever written in public finance.[2]

A whole body of doctrine, extending over a hundred years and including literally hundreds of contributions by scores of scholars, cannot adequately be summarized and critically discussed in a single essay. In spite of this, I shall attempt in this paper to sketch the broad outlines of the Italian tradition, to isolate a few of the important contributions, and to relate these to the present state of fiscal theory.

Procedure

I shall limit my discussion largely to what may properly be called the "classical" Italian tradition in public finance theory. Chronologically, this covers approximately a sixty-year period extending from 1880 to 1940. With the exception of the work of Francesco Ferrara, which is extremely important, although its influence was exerted in an indirect way, I shall not consider precursors of the main figures in Italian thought. I shall not discuss contemporary works of the post World War II period except in so far as these may serve to clarify older contributions and controversies.

After a brief survey of the institutional setting of Italian public finance, I shall first attempt to identify some of the background factors which appear to have exerted some influence on the main Italian ideas and to have produced certain general characteristics in Italian thought. There follows an effort at classifying the Italian works into two broad categories, a classification which is necessarily somewhat incomplete. The second half of the paper begins with the discussion of what I consider to be the important contributions of the Italians. Properly following this, I shall conclude with a summary comparison of the Italian with the Anglo-Saxon tradition.

2. H. C. Simons, *Journal of Political Economy,* XLV (1937), 712-17; F. C. Benham, *Economica,* I (1934), 364-67.

THE INSTITUTIONAL SETTING

Contrary to the conventional practice in England and the United States, the study of public finance in Italy is an independent branch of scholarship. It does not comprise a part of the economics curriculum in the universities; it has a separate curriculum and a separate existence all its own. Normally it is taught and discussed as the science of finance and financial law. Political and legal aspects of finance have been considered integral parts of the discipline, equally important with the economic aspects.

This status has not been entirely a happy one. The doctrinal independence of public finance has been attacked and defended in a continuing controversy. One group, represented by the late Professor Benvenuto Griziotti, has defended the separateness of public finance on the basis of the subject matter. This position follows the Germanic tradition of "Staatswissenschaft." In this view, finance should be studied in its total setting which includes the legal, political, administrative, and economic aspects. These various disciplines are included insofar as they are relevant to the consideration of problems of financing state services. The approach taken by this group has something in common with the American institutionalists, notably with the position of Commons.

The opposing group has tried to emphasize the economic approach to state fiscal activity. While this attitude admits differentiation in the subject of study, it holds that the fundamental distinction should be in method. The importance of the non-economic aspects of fiscal problems is not denied; but proponents of this view are willing to allow these to be considered by non-economists.

The whole controversy over the independence of finance as a separate branch of scholarship has contained much that is sterile. The controversy has, however, served to emphasize certain methodological issues which have been neglected or glossed over in the English-language tradition. These will be discussed in some detail at a later point. But perhaps the most important influence of the doctrinal independence itself has been that public finance, as a branch of scholarship, has attracted many of the better scholars. The science of finance has probably been even more widely respected than general economic theory, and the best Italian economists have felt themselves compelled to do some work in the field. With the single exception of Pareto, who was not without major influence although he was not a direct contributor, all of the outstanding Italian economists have devoted some time to finance theory.

A disadvantage of the doctrinal independence has been that an excessive amount of work has been done in this field relative to others. Although there probably exist external economies to scholarly research in the specific sub-branches of economics, surely the Italians have, in many cases, gone beyond the limits of the full exploitation of such economies. But having established chairs in public finance at many institutions, and having a literal "publish or perish" rule for selection and promotion, Italian scholars have been sometimes forced into relatively unproductive work.

II. BACKGROUND INFLUENCES

Ferrara and the Classical Economics

The influence of classical economics upon Italian fiscal thought cannot be separated from that of Francesco Ferrara. The important classical writings were made available to Italian scholars in translation in the 1850's through the famous series, *Biblioteca dell' economista.* Ferrara selected the works to be translated, supervised the translations, and himself wrote lengthy prefaces to the individual selections. In these prefaces, as in his courses of lectures, Ferrara was intensely critical of many aspects of classical thought. On the whole, his criticisms are excellent by modern criteria, and he anticipated many of the neo-classical contributions. He anticipated, and in some respects surpassed, the subjective-value theorists. He was forceful in his emphasis that value theory must be based on individual behavior, his whole construction departing from what he called "the economic action," the author of such action being the individual who feels, thinks, and wants. The classicists were criticized for their attempts to construct an objective theory of value, and Ferrara was perhaps the first economist completely to shed all of the mercantilist trappings in his rejection of economics as the science of wealth. Value was determined by both utility and cost, with exchange value representing a comparison of these two forces. As a single principle, he developed the idea of the cost of reproduction as a measure of value, meaning by this the cost which would have to be incurred *if* the unit in question were to be reproduced. This principle was extended to apply to goods and services which were not physically reproducible by the introduction of the idea that it is the utility produced by the good, not the good itself, which determines value. Ferrara does not appear to have explicitly discussed diminishing marginal utility as such, although its acceptance is clearly present in his work, as Pareto recognized.[3]

The Physiocratic and classical distinction between productive and unproductive labor was all but demolished by Ferrara. In very persuasive fashion, he showed that the particular form of a good is unimportant, and that immaterial goods or services are equally valuable with material goods. He also rejected the Ricardian rent theory on the basis of a surprisingly modern argument. The idea of differential rent is held to be an undesirable and incorrect heritage of the Physiocratic concept of net product. Rent, or net product, is held to accrue to all factors, not to land alone, and rent, as a distributional share, is attributed to the superior productivity of the productive inputs which receive it.

With this general approach to economic theory, Ferrara was able to reach a profoundly different conception of fiscal activity from that reached by the English classical economists or implied in their works. First of all, he recognizes that social or collective action as well as individual action must be based on individual choice. The state is conceived ideally as a natural outgrowth of the division of labor, and the government is considered as a "producer" of such services as justice, defense, etc. . . . In its pure form, the tax is held to be a payment for such state-supplied services which provide positive utility to the individual.[4] The expenditure

3. V. Pareto, "Per la verità," *Giornale degli economisti* (1895), II, 424. Pareto was an admirer of Ferrara, and traces of much of the Paretian theoretical construction can be found in Ferrara's works.

4. ". . . the tax, in its pure significance, would represent neither a sacrifice nor a violence exercised on the contributor by some superior; it would represent a price . . . for all the great advantages which the state provides for

for these public services may be as productive as that for private goods and services. In this recognition of the tax as a price and of the productivity of public services, the foundation stone for the whole Italian fiscal tradition is laid. The whole of society enjoys the fruits of state services; specific mention is made of schools, port facilities, roads, asylums, and hospitals. It is to the advantage of each citizen to cede a portion of his private goods to the state in exchange for such services.

This broad view of the fiscal process might suggest that Ferrara was less libertarian than the English classicists. Such is, however, not the case. The "economic" conception of fiscal activity was, to Ferrara, an ideal. In the actual state of the world, Ferrara considered that the levy of taxes tended to be oppressive and constituted the "great secret through which tyranny is organized." Although his analysis is not developed in terms of the specific contrast, Ferrara's distinction between the philosophical or "economic" concept of fiscal activity and the historical or "oppressive" concept may also be considered as an early statement of the more refined distinctions which were later to be very important in Italian fiscal thought.[5]

Although recognizing that public services may be productive, Ferrara was intensely critical of the view, which had been expressed by German writers, that merely because tax revenues are transformed into public spending and are returned to the economy, society does not undergo a net loss. He emphasized the necessity for spending the tax proceeds productively, and he constantly referred to the required comparison between utility and cost.[6] The tax is the instrument by which the consumption of one type of good (public) comes to be substituted for another (private). The test of efficiency is always to be found in a comparison of these two consumptions.

---

us." (*Trattato speciale delle imposte* [1849-1850] contained in *Lezioni di economia politica,* [Bologna: 1934], II, 551.)

5. Einaudi has stated that this is the major contribution of Ferrara to fiscal theory. See, Luigi Einaudi, *"Francesco Ferrara,"* in *Saggi bibliografici e storici intorno alle dottrine economiche* (Rome: 1953).

6. "The tax itself is neither a good nor an evil. To make an adequate judgment, one needs to compare the sacrifice with the utility which is promised." (Ferrara, *loc. cit.*, p. 469.)

Interestingly, Ferrara's influence on the development of Italian fiscal thought appears to have been rather indirect. Until the publication of his lectures in 1934, Italian scholars made little reference to his works. Yet the similarity between the basic conceptual framework developed by Ferrara and the subsequent development in Italy suggests that his ideas were instrumental. The explanation is probably provided in the direct influence which Ferrara exerted on the thinking of the early writers, notably Pantaleoni and, through him, on De Viti De Marco. Thus it came to be that subsequent Italian scholars looked to Pantaleoni and De Viti as the sources of their discipline, only to awaken in the 1930's to find that Ferrara had been the genuine fountainhead of ideas.

Regardless of the means through which they were transmitted, Ferrara's ideas muted the impact of the classical implications at precisely those points where these implications could bear on fiscal theory. In Anglo-Saxon fiscal thought, this sort of influence has been absent. Here is explained, at least in part, several important differences in the two developing bodies of fiscal doctrine.[7] It explains why the Italians have from the beginning recognized the spendings side of the fiscal account as an integral part of fiscal activity, whereas, even today, this has not yet been fully incorporated into the English tradition. As a corollary to this, the greater Anglo-Saxon emphasis on sacrifice theories of taxation is more readily understandable. The concept of net sacrifice as a result of the fiscal process has been almost completely absent from Italian works. The Ferrarian influence also explains why the single tax has had little support in Italy.

The Theory of Utility

While the Ferrarian model was influential in taking some of the rougher edges off classical economics, it was equally important through its positive contribution in preparing the groundwork for a ready acceptance of the subjective-value approach and the theory

7. Einaudi, in his review of Pigou's *Study in Public Finance,* makes the telling point that if Ferrara's ideas had been accepted outside of Italy, this would have prevented all such efforts as Pigou's attempted distinction between productive and transfer expenditure. (Luigi Einaudi, *La riforma sociale,* XXXIX [1928], 164.)

of marginal utility. And it is only after Ferrara's major work was completed, and also after the subjective-value decade of the 1870's, that Italian fiscal theory emerged in its fullest sense. The origins of "classical" Italian theory, represented in the works of Pantaleoni and De Viti De Marco, appeared in 1883 and 1888 respectively. These represent attempts to apply the theory of marginal utility to the activity of the public entity. While this attempt to explain state action in terms of the marginal calculus was but natural to the Italian familiar with Ferrara's works, it was foreign and unnatural to the Englishman or the American imbued with Ricardo's principles, and therefore was never carried out.

Interestingly, Pantaleoni first applied the marginal calculus to the theory of public expenditure rather than the theory of taxation. He tried to construct a theory of public spending analogous to the theory of consumption for the individual with the decision-maker being the average or representative member of the legislative assembly. Public revenues were to be distributed among the various possible employments so as to equalize the marginal yields from equivalent units in the minds of the average legislator.

De Viti was more ambitious. He attempted to show that an "economic" theory of the whole fiscal process could be developed. His fundemental early work, *Il carratere teorico del' economia finanziaria* (1888), was conceived independently of the work of Emil Sax which appeared in Austria one year earlier and it is, in many respects, vastly superior to the Sax effort. The stated purpose of De Viti's monograph is that of extending the principles of theoretical economics to fiscal activity. The extension is accomplished by accepting the state as the subject for study in lieu of the individual. The task of the economist is held to be that of studying the behavior of the state in fulfilling its tasks, not that of determining the ends of state activity. While the motives for state action may be different from those of individual action, the overriding principle remains that of "minimum means," and, on this principle, De Viti tried to erect his theory. Public activty is held to be eminently productive, and it serves to satisfy collective needs. But the production of public services is costly, and there is required a comparison of satisfaction and cost; this comparison is the essence of the financial calculus.

The Theory of General Equilibrium

With the work of Pantaleoni and De Viti De Marco in the 1880's, Italian fiscal theory achieved an independent status. As the tradition developed, however, the emerging Walrasian-Paretian work on general equilibrium was to exert substantial influence. This explanation of the economic process served to reinforce the Ferrarian orientation toward generality in approach and to draw attention away from the study of particular problems. Thus, except for an early work by Pantaleoni, the theory of tax shifting and incidence, which was largely born in the Marshallian tradition of partial equilibrium, is relatively unimportant. The general-equilibrium approach exerted further influence in forcing Italian theorists to recognize both sides of the fiscal account. The influence of general-equilibrium analysis on Italian fiscal thought came through an acceptance by the Italian writers of the Walrasian-Paretian construction and not through any direct contribution on the part of Walras or Pareto. Walras constructed his model in abstraction from the state, and Pareto removed collective action from economics by his claim that completely different principles of choice are applicable.

The Theory of the Ruling Class

The fourth major idea or conception which appears to have affected Italian fiscal theory in a significant way is that of the ruling class. This owes its origin to both Mosca and Pareto. The ruling-class conception of government, which was perhaps born out of the Italian political turmoil, has been formulated in almost complete independence of the Marxist conception although clearly the two approaches have much in common. The "ruling class" in Italian political thought need not be historically determined by the laws of production; it can be an hereditary class, an intellectual élite, a political party temporarily in power, or the proletariat. It may be permanent or it may be shifting; it may exert its power through autocratic or democratic forms and institutions. This conception is, therefore, broader and more general than the Marxist. The essential characteristic is the denial of the democratic process in the reaching of social or collective decisions. Social decisions are always made by a group smaller than the total citizenry. The Anglo-Saxon idea of universal participation in the processes of social or collective choice, either directly or through representation, does not appear to have dominated Italian thought or even to have been widely accepted.

The ruling-class conception has forced Italian thinkers, even those who do not accept its validity, to devote greater attention to the form of the state. In this respect the conception has proved to be of great value for the development of fiscal theory. It has made Italian fiscal theorists more explicit as regards their political presuppositions. By contrast, in the non-Italian tradition the political assumptions have rarely been stated with the resultant inherent inconsistencies and contradictions. As Wicksell so acutely noted, the implicit assumption has often been that of benevolent despotism.[8]

Scientism

A final influencing factor in Italian fiscal thought has been the insistence that work in this field remain purely "scientific," or, in current methodological terminology, "positivistic." In the Italian context this characteristic of scholarship is synonomous with objectivity or impartiality, and it carries with it no precise operational connotations. The task of the scholar is solely one of observation; only by a rigorous adherence to the role of the detached observer of the social scene can a genuinely experimental science be constructed. This view, expressed most clearly by Pareto in his works on sociology, has been present in most of the Italian fiscal work.

8. Knut Wicksell, *Finanztheoretische Untersuchungen,* (Jena: Gustav Fischer, 1896). An English translation of the important part of this work has been published in *Classics in the Theory of Public Finance,* ed. R. A. Musgrave and A. T. Peacock (London: Macmillan, 1958).

See also, Pierre Tabatoni, "La rationalité économique des choix financiers dans la théorie contemporaine des finances publiques," *Économie Appliquée,* VIII (1955), 158.

An important recent American book develops an approach to collective decision-making which has much in common with that propounded by the "ruling class" conception. See Anthony Downs, *The Economic Theory of Democracy* (New York: Harper, 1957).

This positivism has been useful in some respects. It has served to eliminate, from the Italian literature, the lengthy normative discussions on fiscal "justice" which have plagued this field of study elsewhere. The net effect of this approach, however, must be judged as negative. No observer of the social scene can remove himself from the observed, and personal and subjective attitudes necessarily color all activity, including the scientific. The Italian scholar, in his attempt to avoid an open admission of this, tended to become enmeshed in excessive generality. And propositions which he presented as explanatory or descriptive turn out, in some cases, to be valid only on the acceptance of his set of values.

By and large, this attempt at positivism has caused Italian fiscal theory to be much further removed from actual policy issues than is the case in either England or the United States. With rare exceptions, the Italians have not been greatly interested in fiscal reforms, or perhaps better stated, they have tried to conceal what interest they have possessed. This appears to have been unfortunate, because it is precisely from an open and direct interest in reform that many new insights have been, and can be, achieved and new truths attained—truths which will fully stand up to the most severe scientific tests.

Barone and Einaudi, among the important figures, appear to have come closer to escaping this debilitating influence. Both extended the scholar's task beyond that of mere intellectual observation and speculation. But no Italian theorist appears to have approached his task on the basis of an outright and explicitly stated set of personal value judgments. The simple recognition that in the social sciences the observer is necessarily among the observed nowhere shines through.

III. PRINCIPAL FEATURES

The Basic Dualism

Perhaps the most important single characteristic of Italian fiscal thought is its dualism. From the contrasting models of the "philosophical" and the "oppressive" states of Ferrara, and the first explicit development in the De Viti De Marco models of the "cooperative" and the "monopolistic" states, Italian contributions can be classified on the basis of the nature of the political entity or, more specifically, on the basis of the location of the decision-making power. The first alternative involves the fundamental premise of democratic choice to the effect that *all* members of the social group participate conceptually in the reaching of collective decisions. This alternative may be called the "cooperative," the "democratic," or the "individualistic," and it stems from the contractual conception of the state itself. As applied to fiscal theory, this approach tends to concentrate on the individual-choice processes and to emphasize the basic similarity between individual behavior in choosing public goods and that in choosing private goods. This has sometimes been labelled the "economic" approach because individual decisions on collective or public goods and services are normally conceived as being ruled by the economizing principles of choice. As Borgatta states, the central hypothesis is simply that "the application of income to the payment of taxes is a particular case of the general law of the allocation of income."[9] The voluntary aspects of fiscal action are stressed, and the tax is considered as a price in the broadest philosophical sense. The general productivity of public services is a central feature. Although he develops his theoretical structure in terms of the two contrasting models, De Viti De Marco is essentially the source of this approach, and his cooperative state model is his standard construct.

His central idea is that in the cooperative state the producers and the consumers of public services are identical. Therefore, it is erroneous to conceive the tax as other than a form of price, a "season ticket." Although he recognizes the inherent struggle among individuals concerning the distribution of the common burden, this is viewed as a problem of political choice-making. The essence of the fiscal action per se is the marginal equivalence between the two sides of the account, which must hold for the totality if not for the specific individual member of the group. De Viti does not attempt to develop a purely "individualistic" theory in the sense of Wicksell and Lindahl, nor does he appear

9. Gino Borgatta, "Prefazione," *Nuova Collana di Economisti,* Vol. IX, *Finanza* (Turin: 1934), p. xxxi.

to have been impressed by the work of Sax and his Italian followers.

Einaudi is the most distinguished follower of De Viti De Marco in this cooperative or democratic tradition, which has not been the dominant one in terms of number of adherents. Fasiani, clearly the most important figure to emerge in the inter-war period, followed De Viti De Marco in the sense that he developed his theory in terms of the contrasting models of the cooperative and the monopolistic state. However, while De Viti De Marco's major stress was placed in the cooperative model, Fasiani's was placed in the monopolistic model.

The alternative model of state activity owes its continuing importance to Pareto and stands directly opposed to the "democratic" model. Ferrara and De Viti conceived society as moving progressively from the tyrannical or monopolistic state toward the democratic and cooperative state. Pareto was successful in shifting completely this evolutionary emphasis. As of any given period of time, a specific group exerts political power and the individual members of the whole group may be classified into two broad categories, the governing and the governed. Fiscal activity is to be explained solely in terms of the behavior of the ruling group. The important figures in this tradition are Puviani, Pareto, Murray, Borgatta, Barone, Fasiani, and Cosciani.

Within this group a further classification may be made. Certain theorists, especially Borgatta, the most direct follower of Pareto, reject any attempt to use economic analysis in the explanation of fiscal activity. To Pareto and to Borgatta state decisions are made by a different sort of calculus, and there is no such thing as a "science of finance" analogous to economic science. The explanation of fiscal activity should be sought instead in the murky science of sociology. This Paretian emphasis led Borgatta to search for a socio-political theory of the fiscal process without much success.[10] This socio-political approach, which is still accepted by some writers in Italy, leads to the vagueness and indeterminancy which surround such concepts as "countervailing

10. Borgatta adopted a different approach when he examined practical problems in fiscal theory. Here he applied economic analysis in the usual sense and neglected his sociology.

power" which have recently been advanced in other connections in the United States.

Another more important group has tried to construct an economic theory of fiscal activity of the ruling class. This group includes Puviani, Barone (for whom the political assumption is relatively unimportant), Fasiani, and Cosciani. This approach has tended to stress the coercive aspects of fiscal choices, and excellent criticisms of the individualistic approach have been advanced. The individual "versus" the state has been the center of the discussion, and the efforts of the state to conceal its activity through the creation of fiscal illusions has been an important part of the analysis. On the other side, the reactions of individuals, singly or in groups, to the fiscal power of the collectivity (the ruling class) have been emphasized.

Both of the above-mentioned variants of the ruling-class conception remain "individualistic" in terms of decision-making. The idea of any *über-individual* or organic decision-maker is explicitly denied. The characteristic feature is that decisions are made by a limited group of individuals, which the system of relationships called "the state" has placed in power, perhaps only temporarily. Little influence is attributed to the actual form of the state or the actual process of choice, and in this respect the vision is closely akin to that of the Marxist.

The genuinely organic conception, in the explicit sense in which the interests of the individual are presumably incorporated in the general social will as embodied in the state, was almost wholly absent from the Italian fiscal literature before the 1930's. During this decade it appeared in the work of Masci, P. Ricca-Salerno and others influenced surely by the dominant Fascist ideology.

Generality

In many respects, "la scienza delle finanze" resembles philosophy more than it does Marshallian economics. The goal of Italian fiscal theorists has been that of providing generalized or philosophical explanations of the fiscal process. Research has been concerned with the "nature of things" rather than with finding operational propositions in the modern scientific sense. Italian scholars have been interested, by and large, in constructing complete, integrated systems, and the criterion for success has been logical consistency rather than usefulness for making predictions, actual or conceptual.

To many of the modern day Italian specialists, this traditional approach appears sterile, and there is now a tendency to admire and to emulate the Anglo-Saxon problem-solving approach. At the forefront of this reaction was Fubini, who, writing in the 1930's, sharply criticized the overly philosophic emphasis, which he attributed to the excessive influence of Ferrara. He contrasted this with the Ricardian-Marshallian tradition which he held to be superior.

In contrast to this understandable and natural reaction on the part of modern day Italian scholars, the philosophical emphasis has a great deal of value for the Anglo-Saxon scholar who has been trained in the Ricardian-Marshallian tradition and who has been substantially influenced, albeit unconsciously in some cases, by pragmatic-institutionalist ideas.

IV. SPECIFIC CONTRIBUTIONS

General Methodology

Because of the influencing factors and the central characteristics noted, Italian fiscal theory is strongest in precisely those areas where Anglo-Saxon theory is weakest, and *vice versa.* If the Italians, on occasion, seem to have overlooked the fundamental purpose of fiscal economics, problem-solving, the English-language scholars have also failed to recognize that the analysis, and thus the solutions of particular problems, is conditioned by the methodological framework. And it is because the Italians have concentrated on general principles, on internally consistent systems, that their work can be of immense value.

From the outset and with a few notable exceptions, Italian fiscal theory has been developed in general-equilibrium terms. For the Italian, fiscal theory is concerned with the activity of the state, and not primarily with that of the individual as he is affected by the fisc. This is true equally for the "economic" and "non-economic" approaches. The theory is rarely individualistic in the sense that the individual or private economy is the central subject of the analysis.

The general-equilibrium aspects are more inclusive than a mere superimposition of taxes and expenditures onto a Walrasian model. The Italian model includes the state, and the more important feature has been the tying-together of the two sides of the state fiscal account, taxation and expenditure, and the general recognition of the limited usefulness of any one-sided analysis.[11] It is but natural that this feature should stem from the so-called "economic" approach (De Viti De Marco, Einaudi). But somewhat surprisingly it is also accepted by those who specifically reject the economic aspects of fiscal choice (notably Borgatta).[12]

Pantaleoni held that in so far as the tax exceeds that which the individual would freely sacrifice for the public service, the results of taxation were identical to those of brigandage or plunder. De Viti and Einaudi, through the development of their productivity theory of state expenditure, showed that the Pantaleoni view of a tax could be applied only to an individual or group. For the whole community the estimated net benefits must be at least equal to the costs, or the public service would never be performed under the assumption of any sort of rational choice-making for the collectivity.

Perhaps some credence may be given to the claims of the semanticists here, for it seems that by an extremely fortunate choice of words, Einaudi did much to overthrow the brigandage conception of the tax. He labeled the assumption which neglects the effects of the expenditure that of the "imposta grandine." Literally translated, "grandine" means hailstorm. The tax must be considered as something which destroys economic resources or otherwise removes them from the economy once and for all, without further repercussions or effects. By thus laying bare the implications of fiscal analysis limited to the tax side alone, Einaudi was

11. As Del Vecchio has stated: "The history of the science has proved that theoretically there is no possibility of applying partial theories to the science of finance. Any finance problem, even particular ones, presupposes the whole system of economic relationships." (Gustavo Del Vecchio, *Introduzione alla finanza* [Padua: 1954], p. 10).

12. See Gino Borgatta, "Contributi alla teoria della spesa dell imposta," *Studi in memoria di Guglielmo Masci* (Milan: 1943), I, 29-46.

instrumental in forcing Italian theorists to devote specific attention to this aspect of fiscal methodology.

The analysis of the spendings side corollary with that of the tax side was systematically incorporated into the treatment of De Viti De Marco. In his criticism of the traditional doctrine which neglected the effects of spending, De Viti perhaps went too far. For just as the traditional doctrine had unconsciously employed assumptions applicable, if at all, only to partial-equilibrium problems, De Viti conceived the fiscal process only in its most general framework. Here the tax can best be considered as a "price," but he failed to recognize the tremendous difficulties involved in any complete integration of the tax and expenditure sides, and his specific analyses are often oversimplified. De Viti failed to recognize the usefulness of the "imposta-grandine" assumption in analyses aimed only at partial-equilibrium results.

It remained for Fasiani and Cosciani to complete the Italian methodological contribution.[13] Fasiani attempted to identify those cases in which the "imposta-grandine" assumption could be legitimately employed, correctly stating that the real test was the fruitfulness in allowing accurate predictions to be made, not the correspondence of the assumption to apparent reality.

The most important and relevant of these cases were (1) when the purpose is that of deliberately isolating partial effects with the incompleteness fully acknowledged; and (2) when the tax is small and the proceeds are spread over many items of expenditure as opposed to the concentrated effects of the tax. The second case is, of course, the traditionally-assumed setting for partial-equilibrium tax analysis, and many useful results have been obtained from this model. However, this model or framework has also been used to reach general-equilibrium conclusions and this has been the source of much error and confusion. One of the most familiar examples of this is, of course, the so-called "excess burden" analysis which compares the effects of an income tax and

13. Mauro Fasiani, "A proposito di un recente volume sull' incidenza delle imposte," *Giornale degli economisti,* XVIII (1940), 1-23; "Sulla legittimità dell' ipotesi di un imposta-grandine nello studio della ripercussione dei tributi," *Studi in memoria di Guglielmo Masci* (Milan: 1943), I, 261-79; Cesare Cosciani, *Principii di scienza delle finanze* (Turin: 1953), 326-31.

an excise tax. Another is the analysis which attempts to trace the influence of general excise taxes on product prices. Only in the postwar period have economists come to recognize the extreme limitations which must be placed on partial-equilibrium analysis if it is to be useful and to attempt to place their analyses in a more general setting. Precisely because of this welcome shift in perspective, the Italian contribution should only now come to exert its proper influence in fiscal theory. If general equilibrium or general welfare conclusions are sought, Fasiani's second case no longer is an appropriate one, for in "macro-economic" or "income" terms the summed effect of the use of the tax yield in many different expenditure categories will be dimensionally equal to the concentrated effect of the tax levy. Therefore, the expenditure side must be reintroduced. There remains only the first case, that in which no conclusions can be reached at all, except on an acknowledged preliminary basis, conclusions which are, perhaps, better not even published if the ultimate purpose is that of influencing policy decisions in any desirable way. If fiscal theory is to be of any real usefulness in solving problems of political economy, the Italian conception of the fiscal process must perforce be employed.[14]

PUBLIC SERVICES AS PRODUCTIVE FACTORS

Many of the more specific contributions which Italian fiscal theory contains are derivative from the general methodological approach. One of these is the recognition of the general productivity of public expenditure, a contribution which has been developed by those who adopt the "economic" conception of fiscal activity, notably by De Viti De Marco and Einaudi. The essential idea was present in Ferrara but it remained for De Viti to develop it and to use it as a basis for a principle of taxation.

The De Viti vision of public services goes beyond the mere acknowledgment of the usefulness of such services in a general and unspecified sort of way. Many students accept this view, but still conceive public services as *consumption* services, similar in

14. Any model which incorporates some recognition of offsetting changes, for example in the level of alternative taxes or in the absolute price level, should be classified as equivalent methodologically to the Italian model.

many respects to bread and buttermilk. While such services may or may not be essential for existence, it is difficult to impute to them a share in the income-creating or productive processes of the economy. De Viti looked at public services differently; to him these were productive services, that is, inputs in the whole productive operation of the economic mechanism. Public services are instrumental to the production of final goods and are on an equal basis with labor and capital. Therefore, it becomes conceptually possible to impute to such services an appropriate distributive share.

If the productive contribution of such services is specific to particular types of activity, these services will be priced in the ordinary manner. It is only when the contribution is not differential among the separate activities that the fiscal problem in a real sense arises. The existence of the tax rather than the price indicates that the contribution of the services so financed is general for all income-producing activity. Therefore, the properly imputed share owing to the publicly-supplied input is equal for each unit of income produced. As he put it, each unit of real income is born with a tax claim against it. From this it follows that if some units of income should escape this tax claim, other units must necessarily be charged with more than their properly imputed share of government cost.

This argument is more subtle than it at first appears, and it represents perhaps the most complete attempt to develop a purely economic theory of public activity. Its validity depends, however, on the acceptance of either one of two specific assumptions. Either all public services that affect different lines of activity differently must be assumed to be financed by direct pricing arrangements, or, alternatively, the differential effects exerted on each line of activity must be assumed to be mutually canceling when all public services are considered. Neither of these assumptions seems to be empirically supportable. If either one of them should prove to be realistic, however, the De Viti approach might prove acceptable. It could then with some legitimacy be argued that the ideal tax system is one that subtracts an equal share from each unit of income produced, that is, a purely proportional income tax.

Going beyond the distribution of the tax payment, a means is also provided for the determination of the aggregate amount of public activity. The necessary condition is provided in the equality between the marginal productivity of the public services and the marginal productivity of the resources in private employments. Conceptually, the test for this condition is a simple one. Would real income of the community increase, decrease, or remain unchanged by an incrementally small variation in the amount of government activity? Or, to state the criterion more correctly, would the present value of the community's future income stream be increased, decreased, or remain unchanged by an incrementally small change in the amount of government? It should be noted that the evaluation of real income here need not involve any assigning of values to the public services. This problem is eliminated by the device of assuming that these are purely instrumental and that their value shows up in final goods and services.

The grand design of De Viti was thus to apply the marginal-productivity theory of distribution to the fiscal problem. This theory is, however, an explanation of the workings of the private market economy, given the appropriate institutional framework. Resources will tend to be paid in accordance with their marginal productivity. But the extension of this sort of analysis to the fiscal problem introduces another dimension. There is nothing inherent in the workings of the collective choice-making process to cause the marginal-productivity criteria to be met. This is the great failure of the De Viti model. If, in fact, individuals could respond voluntarily in their purchases of public services, some such theory might provide an explanation. Separate individuals might freely choose the margin between the public and the private employment of resources. But what De Viti failed to see is that, despite the objectivity with which real income might conceptually be measured, this is not the appropriate criterion upon which private individuals will choose. Given any assumed value scale, real income for the community may conceptually be measured. But it is the distribution of such income among individuals which is relevant for individual choices. The criterion of social real income can be made objectively meaningful only if the decision-making power is located in some particular individual, group, or class who chooses to accept this criterion. Once this is admitted, the productivity conception loses much of its appeal and merit.[15]

De Viti's theory can only be rescued if it is changed into a normative one. It must be presumed to define a goal toward which collective action should strive. This involves the acceptance of certain value judgments concerning social welfare. It must state that the only correct evaluation of real income is that provided by the currently existing value scale established. Thus the De Viti attempt to apply the marginal-productivity theory of distribution to the fiscal problem goes beyond the mere acceptance of marginal-productivity payments as the ethically justified system of distribution for the private economy. It proposes to extend this norm to the public economy as well.

If the De Viti analysis is considered as explanatory, it is open to objections on analytical grounds; if it is considered as normative it need not be accepted on ethical grounds. In spite of this, the approach is highly useful because of the insights it offers. First of all, it indicates that if specific public services are really in the nature of productive inputs and do affect certain lines of production differentially, the allocation of economic resources will tend to be affected adversely unless such public services are directly priced. The direction as well as the degree of resource distortion will vary in each case, depending upon, among other things, the elasticity of demand for the final product in question. Only within the last few years has this point come to be widely recognized; only recently has it been made clear that if we do not "price" highway services properly we shall get too many resources devoted to automotive transportation; if we do not "price" the services of firemen we shall get too little investment in fire protection devices, etc.

The De Viti conception also offers interesting insights on the whole idea of the neutral fiscal system. In the English-American tradition, strongly influenced by Pigou, the neutral tax system is supposed to require a set of lump-sum taxes. Any other system will have positive announcement effects. It is obvious that this line

15. This point is made by Papi. See G. U. Papi, *Equilibrio fra attività economia e finanziaria* (Milan: 1942) p. 17.

of thought stems directly from an undue concentration on the tax side to the neglect of the expenditure side. The De Viti approach indicates that the neutral tax structure is dependent upon the distribution of expenditures which is assumed, and that neutrality can be defined only in terms of both sides of the fiscal account.

Einaudi's conception of public activity closely follows that of De Viti. He suggests that the "optimal" tax, defined as that which leads to the maximum production of real income for the community, is that which bears on each particle of real income equally.[16] His treatment is superior to that of De Viti, however, in that his analysis per se does not depend upon his conception of the fiscal process. He explicitly states his principle of equality as a normative statement for the distribution of taxation. Each particle of real income, defined in the flow sense, *should* be equally taxed. His conclusions follow from this premise. Einaudi is almost alone among the Italians in adopting this methodological procedure.

Critique of Sacrifice Theories

As the discussion of the previous section indicates, the Italian approach can perhaps contribute more in a negative or critical sense that it can in any positive way. We find the Italians assuming the front ranks among the critics of the sacrifice "theories" of taxation, normative "theories" or "principles" which have dominated the Anglo-Saxon tradition, and which remain influential enough to justify whole works being written to dispel them.[17] No important Italian theorist has advanced propositions of the Mill, Edgeworth, Cohen-Stuart, Pigou type, which state that the best tax system is achieved when individual sacrifices are equal or equi-proportional or when aggregate sacrifice is minimized. The Italian contribution has been rather in excellent critiques of these propositions, for the Italians follow the developments in the Eng-

16. Cf. Luigi Einaudi, "Contributo alla ricerca dell' ottima imposta," *Annali di economia,* V (1929).

17. The recent study by Walter J. Blum and Harry Kalven, Jr., *The Uneasy Case for Progressive Taxation* (Chicago: 1953) is largely devoted to an attack on the sacrifice theories. And, although fiscal theorists might consider the argument as flogging a dead horse, the fact that the book was published and has received favorable reviews in the professional journals is sufficient proof of the point made in the text.

lish-language publications quite closely. Notable critics are Barone and Einaudi, both of whom wrote on this subject as early as 1912.

Barone, always a clear thinker, was at his best when he demolished all versions of the sacrifice principle.[18] He applied essentially the same reasoning to all versions. The principle was invalid for two reasons. First, the utility of income for Tizio is not comparable with that of Caio. Second, even neglecting the problem of inter-personal comparability, a general pattern of tax distribution could be indicated only if the utility functions for the individuals were found to be of specific forms. By modification of the shapes of these functions, a progressive, proportional, or regressive tax system could be justified. As for the Edgeworth principle of minimum aggregate sacrifice, Barone acknowledged its superiority over the others in its being neat and precise both in its premises and in its conclusions. He showed, however, that this principle also required the comparability of utilities among individuals. But he went further and asked the question: Does the principle really minimize aggregate *social* sacrifice? Redistributive measures may be applied, without apparent harm to the social structure, in the short run, but the results may well be different if longer run considerations are taken into account. Finally Barone concluded: "This doctrine of minimum sacrifice represents one of the major aberrations which may be reached by the arbitrary calculus of pleasure and pain."[19]

Barone concluded further that all theories of taxation based in any way on the marginal utility of income to the individual are inadequate and purely arbitrary. A system of taxation should be clear and predictable, and it should not be made to depend on the particular psyche of the individual which cannot possibly be examined in any objective way.

The Barone critique is substantially complete, and today, some forty-five years after it was written, it remains superior to

18. Enrico Barone, *Le opere economiche,* Vol. III, *Principii di economia finanziaria* (Bologna: 1937), pp. 149-60. The relevant portions of this work were originally published in *Giornale degli economisti* (1912).

19. *Ibid.,* p. 158.

all but a handful of contributions in the Anglo-Saxon literature.

Einaudi developed a critical argument on much the same grounds in his course of lectures in 1910-1911 which were not published.[20] Starting with a simplified arithmetical model which shows how the assumption of a diminishing marginal utility of income could lead to an argument for progressive taxation, Einaudi then asks: Is it possible to sum utilities over separate individuals? He answers by stating that the sacrifices are individualized sensations which each person is able to measure and compare, but that it is impossible to add the sensations of Tizio and Caio. The minimum sacrifice principle is, therefore, of no significance.

Italian fiscal thought has never been plagued with the heritage of utilitarianism which has so influenced the development of fiscal theory in England and America. The minimum sacrifice principle, and its more ambiguous cousin, the ability-to-pay principle, is still a part of our fiscal doctrine. Perhaps the latter principle owes its popularity to its very ambiguity; it can be used to criticize, or alternatively to support, almost an infinite number of distributions of the tax load.

Tax Capitalization

One contribution that is peculiarly attributable to Professor Luigi Einaudi and which also stems directly from the productivity conception of public activity is contained in the analysis of tax capitalization. Einaudi was successful in overthrowing the so-called "classical" views. This was accomplished in a series of essays written between 1912 and 1934.[21] The "classical" or orthodox view held that whereas a partial tax was subject to capitalization, a general tax was not due to the effects of the general tax upon the rate of interest. Italian representatives of this theory were Gobbi and Ricci.[22] This view was discussed in America

20. He repeats his argument in Einaudi, "Il cosidetto principio della imposta produttivista," *La riforma sociale* (1933). Reprinted in *Saggi sul risparmio e l'imposta* (Turin: 1941), pp. 286-88.

21. These essays are all reprinted, along with others, in Luigi Einaudi, *Saggi sul risparmio e l'imposta* (Turin: 1941).

22. Cf. U. Gobbi, *Trattato di economia,* 2nd ed. (Milan: 1923), II, p. 129; U. Ricci, "La taxation de l'épargne," *Revue d'économie politique,* XVI (1927), 878-79.

some forty years ago by T. S. Adams and E. R. A. Seligman, and it has recently been advanced again in a series of articles by J. A. Stockfisch.[23]

Einaudi correctly showed that the orthodox view on tax capitalization depended upon the acceptance of the "imposta-grandine" assumption concerning the other side of the fiscal account. He showed that, if the government's use of the tax proceeds is taken into account, the effects of the rate of interest may be different in different situations depending on the relative efficiency of government's use of the revenues.

The dominant theory stated that if the tax covered an important field of resource return—that is, if the tax was of the type usually referred to as "general"—it must exert some effect on the rate of yield on capital resources. If completely general, the tax will reduce the rate of yield on all earning assets. This would appear to affect capital values; but when it is recalled that capital values are determined by both the yield and the rate of interest, the simple conclusion does not follow. For, accepting a productivity theory of interest-rate determination, the capitalization rate is reduced *pari-passu* with the yield. Therefore, capital values remain unchanged.

Einaudi did not accept this theory, and he showed that it contained the standard fiscal fallacy of neglecting the effects of the expenditure of the tax revenues. Presumably the government plans to use its tax revenues. If so, then the effects upon the rate of interest cannot be determined *a priori*. Einaudi said that if the funds were used as advantageously by the state as they would have been if left in private hands, the real income of the community will not change, and the rate of interest will tend to remain unchanged. Thus, the general tax will tend to be capitalized. Capital values will be reduced.

23. J. A. Stockfisch, "The Capitilization and Investment Aspects of Excise Taxes Under Competition," *American Economic Review,* XLIV (1954), 287-300; "The Capitalization, Allocation, and Investment Effects of Asset Taxation," *Southern Economic Journal,* XXII (1956), 316-29. See my, "The Capitalization and Investment Aspects of Excise Taxes under Competition: Comment," *American Economic Review,* XLVI (December 1956), 974-77, for an application of Einaudi's argument to the Stockfisch analysis.

On the other hand, if the state uses the funds more advantageously than they would have been used in private employments, a premise of the economic theory of state activity, real income of the community would be increased. Additional savings would be forthcoming, and probably the rate of interest would diminish. As a third possibility, the state may use the proceeds of the tax in some manner less efficient than would be the case if the funds were left in private employments. In this case, the community's real income would be diminished. Savings would be reduced, and presumably the rate of interest would be increased. Thus, if the "grandine" assumption is fully accepted, said Einaudi, the conclusions drawn from the orthodox theory are wrong. Griziotti, in an important early article, substantially supported and reinforced the Einaudi thesis.[24]

The details of the Einaudi-Griziotti argument need not be accepted to recognize the value of this contribution, which reduces to an application of the Italian methodological position to the particular problem of tax capitalization. The error in the orthodox position on tax capitalization regarding the impossibility of capitalizing a general tax stems from the failure to extend the analysis to a genuinely general equilibrium framework. The effects of a generally-imposed tax on resource yields is fully acknowledged; and the effect of the level of resource yields on interest rate determination is also accepted. But the analysis stops one step short of the necessary generality. It must also include the effect of the expenditure of the proceeds on the rate of yield. In its most basic sense, Einaudi is stating that there can be no truly general tax. All income-producing sources cannot be simultaneously hit because government is also an income-producing source. The fiscal process is essentially a two-sided, balance sheet sort of affair.

The Double Taxation of Savings

As mentioned above, Einaudi was one of the few Italian writers who explicitly stated a value premise at the start of his analysis.

24. Benvenuto Griziotti, "Teoria dell' ammortamento delle imposte e sue applicazione," *Giornale degli economisti* (1918), reprinted in *Studi di scienza delle finanze e diritto finanziario* (Milan: 1956), II, 275-391.

This was that each particle of income *should* be taxed equally. A significant portion of his work has been devoted to showing that the tax on personal income levied *in the ordinary way* does not meet this criterion. This argument involved an elaboration of the J. S. Mill-Irving Fisher thesis that the inclusion of income saved in the tax base involves double taxation. Therefore, Einaudi concludes, equity requires the exemption of income saved.[25]

A considerable portion of the Einaudi argument is simply arithmetic. He shows, clearly and precisely, that the present value of a specific amount of income devoted to saving (capital formation) becomes less than the present value of an equivalent amount of income devoted to current consumption if the income from the capital created is also to be taxed. The only way in which the present values of such equivalent units of current income can be equated is by the exemption of savings from current taxation. This is the only means by which savings can be prevented from being taxed twice, once originally as income and secondly on its yield.[26]

The close relation between this argument and the Einaudi argument on tax capitalization discussed above should be mentioned. If, in fact, the classical argument on the capitalization of a general tax were acceptable, there would be no double taxation of savings. For, if taxation did not serve to reduce capital values, there would be no difference in the present values of like amounts of income devoted to savings and to consumption.

Although Einaudi has not been without his supporters, notably Fasiani, the double taxation of savings thesis has not been widely accepted in Italy. The primary influence seems to have been that of De Viti De Marco who employed his own version of the productivity of state services to overthrow the Einaudi argument, much to the surprise of Einaudi. In its most general sense the totality of public services is considered by De Viti as a factor entering into the production of all economic goods and services, that is, all real income. Therefore, each portion of income has a tax

25. The main Einaudi works on this point are included in the volume cited above, *Saggi sul risparmio e l'imposta,* and in "Contributo alla ricerca dell' ottima imposta," *Annali di economia,* V (1929).

26. The Einaudi thesis has been made forcefully by Nicholas Kaldor. See his *An Expenditure Tax* (London: Allen and Unwin, 1955).

claim against it. Recognizing this, it is erroneous to impute the whole of a future income stream to a current private investment of capital. The capital is productive due to the aid of the state environment; therefore, a portion of future income is to be attributed to public productive services. It follows that all units of current income must be fully taxed in order to compensate the state for its contribution; but it also follows that all units of future income must also be taxed. In other words, De Viti said that equality in present values is not the proper criterion for tax equity. He said that incomes of each period must be considered separately for tax purposes. Einaudi argued that capital and income are simply different dimensions of the same magnitudes. De Viti implied that this would be true only in an economy without the state. If the state is introduced, capital and income are not merely different in a dimensional sense; income carries with it a tax claim.

Thus taxing income as earned and then the yield on that portion saved does not involve double taxation at all, but is, on the contrary, necessary in order to achieve objective equality in the treatment of all income units.

In this rather ingenious way, De Viti was able to overcome the force of the tautological exactness of the Einaudi position. Although consistently holding an *"ertrag"* concept of income, he arrived at conclusions similar in many respects to those produced by the use of the *"einkommen"* concept.[27]

The Italian Contribution to Debt Theory[28]

The theory of public debt has been a central issue in Italian fiscal theory, and the contributions of Italian scholars are sufficiently unique, both in approach and analysis, to warrant a special discussion. The issue, in effect the debate, has been drawn almost exclusively in terms of the basic Ricardian proposition concerning the fundamental equivalence between extraordinary taxes and public loans.

27. Cf. Henry Simons, *Personal Income Taxation* (Chicago: University of Chicago Press, 1938).

28. The discussion of this section closely parallels that contained in my *Public Principles of Public Debt* (Homewood: Irwin, 1958), Ch. 8, Appendix.

The Ricardian thesis was elaborated and extended by De Viti De Marco.[29] Ricardo argued that the fully rational individual should be indifferent as between paying an extraordinary tax of $2,000 once-and-for-all and paying an annual tax of $100 in perpetuity, assuming an interest rate of 5 per cent. He extended this analysis to apply to all individuals, and concluded that if the government borrows $2,000 and commits taxpayers to finance interest payments of $100 annually, the individual living in a future income period would find himself in an identical position with that which he would have enjoyed had the government chosen to impose the extraordinary tax of $2,000. The individual will fully capitalize the future tax payments when the debt is created, and he will write down the capital value of the income-earning assets which he owns by the present value of these future tax payments.

The limited life span of the individual does not affect the analysis. If an individual pays the once-and-for-all extraordinary tax, his heirs will receive capital assets reduced in value by this amount. If, on the other hand, the debt is created, his heirs will receive capital assets yielding a higher gross income. But when the interest charge is deducted, the net income stream is identical with that received in the tax situation.

The analysis would, at first glance, appear to apply only for those individuals possessing patrimony or capital. Its extension to individuals, members of professional or laboring groups, who own no income-earning assets is not initially evident. But Ricardo, and De Viti De Marco, anticipated this and made this extension. The individual who possesses no capital assets which he can sell to raise funds to meet his extraordinary tax obligation must of necessity borrow privately, thereby obligating himself to meet future interest charges on a private debt. In this case, provided only that the interest rates on the public and the private debts are the same, the individual owes an equivalent interest charge in each future period. The effect of the government's replacing

29. Antonio De Viti De Marco, "La pressione tributaria dell' imposta e del prestito," *Giornale degli economisti* (1893) I, 38-67, 216-31. Essentially the same analysis is contained in *First Principles of Public Finance,* tr. E. P. Marget (New York: 1936), pp. 377-98.

the extraordinary tax with the public loan is nothing more than the replacement of a whole set of private loan arrangements with the public loan.[30]

It is at this point that Ricardo as well as De Viti De Marco became confused. Accepting the restrictive assumptions necessary for the analysis to be valid, how does this analysis affect the question as to whether the burden of the debt is shifted forward in time? Both Ricardo and De Viti suggested that the full burden of the debt must rest on individuals living at the time of debt creation.

But how may the "burden" of the debt be defined? In one sense we may define it as the sacrifice of goods and services which could have been consumed if the public expenditure which the debt financed had not been undertaken. It is clear that burden in this sense must rest on individuals living in future generations. They are the individuals who must sacrifice a portion of their income for debt service which they otherwise could have consumed. And the fact that bondholders receive the interest payments on internal debt does not modify this conclusion. If, however, the burden of the debt is defined in this manner, how can individuals living in future time periods be in equivalent positions in the two situations, with the debt and with the extraordinary tax. The answer can only be that individuals living in future time periods *must also bear the real burden of the extraordinary tax under the narrowly restrictive Ricardian-De Vitian assumptions.* It is true that, under these assumptions, the effects of the loan and the extraordinary tax are equivalent, but the correct inference is that the real burden of both is passed on to future time periods, not that this burden is borne in both cases by the individuals living during the initial period.

This rather paradoxical conclusion may be readily seen when the nature of the extraordinary tax required to make the Ricardian proposition hold is examined. Both Ricardo and De Viti assumed that such a tax would either be drawn wholly from privately-held capital assets, that is to say, that individuals would sell off capital

30. The most complete statement of Ricardo's position is to be found in: *Principles of Political Economy and Taxation, Works and Correspondence* (London: Royal Economic Society, 1951), I, 244-46.

holdings sufficiently to finance the tax obligation, or they would create private debts (incur capital liabilities) to the full amount of the individual share of the tax. In other words, the extraordinary tax was to be a capital levy *in fact,* regardless of the form which the fiscal authority chooses. If the full amount of the tax is financed from capital, then it becomes clear that the current generation does not suffer any real income reduction. The current generation essentially "draws on capital" in the form of the public project undertaken.

The failure to grasp this point appears to have been fundamental, but the reason for this is not difficult to find. The individuals who are coercively forced to give up resources, whether these are drawn from consumption or investment uses, are normally considered to "bear" the costs of the project financed. Taxes, of any sort, are held to impose a sacrifice on individuals during the period when the tax obligations must be met. This becomes a reasonable, and correct, inference when it is recognized that the ownership of capital assets itself provides some utility to the individual. This being the case, we can say that regardless of the source of the funds paid out in taxes, the individual undergoes a "sacrifice" of utility. It may also be claimed that, if individuals fully discount future tax obligations, the creation of future interest payments on a debt reduces the present value of an expected utility stream. Thus, both the extraordinary tax and the public debt of like amount must be "paid" by individuals during the time of the original transaction.

Thus, we have reached diametrically opposing conclusions; first we stated that the burden of both the extraordinary tax and the public loan rests, under the Ricardian-De Vitian assumptions, exclusively on individuals living in future time periods. This conclusion holds when we consider burden in terms of sacrificed real goods and services. Secondly, we stated that the burden of both the extraordinary tax and the public loan rests, under the full Ricardian-De Vitian assumptions, on the individuals living during the initial period. This conclusion holds when we try to measure sacrifice or burden in terms of the change in present value of an expected or anticipated utility stream, and when we attribute some positive utility to the holding of income-earning assets.

The confusion of these two concepts becomes especially likely when it is recognized that the actual form of any conceivable tax levy, either extraordinary or normal, must differ from the Ricardian model in the direction which adds to the confusion. The Ricardian model overlooks the essential difference between the coercive levy of taxes and the voluntary subscription to public loans. Any coercive imposition of a tax seems certain to reduce both current consumption spending and investment spending. The assumption that only the latter is affected, that is, only private capital formation is reduced (private liability formation increased), is clearly incorrect. If we make the assumption that an individual attempts at any point in time to attain some marginal equalization between the present value of expected future enjoyments of income and the present value of current enjoyments of income, then any tax imposition will cause him to adjust both types of outlay downward. Some portion of any tax must come from current consumption spending, whatever the form that this tax takes. This being the case, some share of the extraordinary tax comes to rest on individuals living in the initial period, even if we consider only the real aspects and ignore the utility aspects altogether. On the other hand, the public loan operates through voluntary subscription. Individuals are likely to reduce current consumption outlay only in so far as the interest rate encourages an increased rate of saving, a questionable relationship. The major share of funds going into the purchase of government securities does come from private capital formation. The generation of individuals currently living sacrifices nothing in utility and little, if anything, in real goods and services in creating the loan. Therefore, in the real sense, there is a differential effect between the extraordinary tax and the public loan.

This differential effect is further widened when it is recognized that the full Ricardian assumptions do not hold on the utility side either. Individuals do not fully discount future tax payments. If the Ricardian-De Vitian reasoning is accepted for all individuals owning capital assets and receiving sufficient income to allow them to borrow privately, there still may be other large groups of individuals. These comprise the bulk of the lower income or laboring classes. It is impossible to levy extraordinary taxes on these individuals. The extraordinary tax must be levied on the first two groups. But, if the public debt is created, some portion of the annual interest charges may be placed on the third group. The lower income classes in future time periods may bear a portion of the burden of the public loan whereas they must, by definition, escape fully the burden of the extraordinary tax. This is the objection which Griziotti raised to the De Viti elaboration of the Ricardian thesis.[31]

De Viti De Marco attempted to refute this objection, but he was not really successful. He tried to show that even the complete exemption of all non-propertied individuals from the extraordinary tax would not affect his conclusions. Here he introduced a long-run competitive model. He reasoned that such exemption would tend to increase the relative attractiveness of the professional non-propertied occupations. This would, in turn, cause more people to enter these occupations and to turn away from those activities such as management and administration of property. In the long run, the lot of the non-propertied classes would tend to be identical with that which they would enjoy even if they were taxed for the service of the public loan. As Griziotti suggested, this represents the stretching of the competitive model a bit too far.

Griziotti went further and argued that, even for individuals owning capital assets, discounting of future tax payments does not take place fully. Individuals do not act as if they live forever, and familial lines are not treated as being continuous. There is nothing sacred about maintaining capital intact, and individuals will not necessarily do so. The equivalence hypothesis requires continued abstinence from consuming capital on the part of those holding capital assets after public debt is created. Whereas the extraordinary tax effectively removes from an individual's possibilities the capital sum (once he has paid the tax he can no longer convert at least that portion of his capital into income), the

31. Benvenuto Griziotti, "La diversa pressione tributaria del prestito e dell' imposta," *Giornale degli economisti* (1917). Reprinted in *Studi di scienza delle finanze e diritto finanziario* (Milan: 1956), II, 193-261.

disposition over this capital remains in his power in the public debt case. He may convert this capital into income at any time, without in any way removing the tax obligation on his heirs which is necessitated by the debt service.

Griziotti's claim that the creation of public debts does involve a shifting of the tax burden forward in time was not successful in overcoming the dominance of the De Viti De Marco elaboration of the Ricardian thesis in Italy. The prestige and apparent logical clarity of the De Vitian argument coupled with the changed conditions were successful in reducing the Griziotti influence. There have been isolated supporters of Griziotti,[32] but the De Viti formulation continues to dominate the Italian scene.

Additional elements of the De Viti De Marco conception of public debt may be mentioned since he anticipated much of the "new orthodoxy," which came to be adopted in the United States only after the Keynesian revolution. To anticipate erroneous ideas is, of course, no great contribution, but De Viti's arguments concerning the problem of debt repayment are surprisingly modern in this respect. Included in his discussion of the public debt is what he called the theory of automatic amortization. De Viti used this to demonstrate that debt should never be repaid. De Viti started from his interpretation of the Ricardian argument that public debt merely serves as a substitute for private debts. He assumes a community of three individuals, only one of whom is a capitalist.[33] Now assume that the state requires a sum of 1,200,000 and levies an extraordinary tax, 400,000 on each individual. Individual 1 being the capitalist, individuals 2 and 3 will find it necessary to borrow from him in order to meet their tax obligations paying an assumed interest rate of 5 per cent. As these individuals save in future periods, they may amortize their debt to the capitalist.

Now assume that the government, instead of levying the tax, borrows the 1,200,000 directly from Individual 1. The annual interest charge will be 60,000, and it is assumed to collect 20,000

32. For example, see F. Maffezzoni, "Ancora della diversa pressione tributaria del prestito e dell' imposta," *Rivista di diritto finanziario e scienza delle finanze,* IX (1950), 341-75.

33. This argument is developed in *First Principles of Public Finance,* pp. 390-93.

from each of the three citizens. As in the first case, as individuals 2 and 3 save they may utilize this savings to purchase the government securities, which are assumed to be marketable, from Individual 1. Their purchase of government securities in this case is identical in effect to their paying off private debts in the other case. Therefore, as the government securities are widely circulated among the population the real debt is more or less automatically amortized. Individuals in purchasing debt instruments acquire an asset to offset their tax liabilities. The weight of the debt is effectively destroyed; hence debt need never be repaid and there need be no fear that a country cannot bear the burden of public debts, however heavy these might appear to be.

This construction is both ingenious and misleading. Let us consider the private borrowing case carefully. Individuals 2 and 3, as they accumulate savings, increase their net worth, and they must also increase some item on the asset side, let us say, cash. When they accumulate sufficient cash to warrant paying off a portion of the private debt, the transaction is represented on their balance sheets as a drawing down of the cash item and a corresponding drawing down of their liability item. *Net worth does not change with debt repayment.*[34]

The construction is identical with the public loan. As individuals accumulate savings these must take some form, cash, savings accounts, etc. Net worth is increased along with whatever asset item the individual chooses to put his savings into. At one point we assume that the individual accumulates sufficient funds to purchase a debt instrument. In so doing, he reduces his cash item and increases another asset item, government securities. He has, in this particular transaction, merely transformed one asset into another. *His net worth is not modified.* Therefore, the weight of having to pay the annual tax upon the debt instrument is precisely as heavy after as before his acquisition of the security.

De Viti De Marco is correct, in the extremes of his model, in saying that this transaction is equivalent to the repayment of private loans. In this sense the public debt is said to be amortized. But his error lies in inferring from this that public debt should not

34. Cf. F. Maffezzoni, "Ancora della diversa pressione tributaria del prestito e dell' imposta," *op. cit.*, p. 348.

be repaid in fact. This error is based upon a misunderstanding of private loans. Implicit in the De Viti formulation is the idea that the repayment of private loans is necessarily beneficial to the individual. De Viti assumed that such repayment increases private net worth, and thereby reduces the weight or "pressure" of the loan. He failed to see that the new savings which go into private debt repayment have alternative employments. Whether or not private debt repayment reduces "pressure" on the individual economy, depends solely upon the relative rates of return.

The same is true for public debt. Having demonstrated that the transfer of public debt instruments might be similar in some models to private debt repayment, De Viti inferred that this "amortization" reduces the pressure or weight of the public debt. This is not necessarily true at all. The weight of debt remains as it was before, and the purchase of government securities can modify this only in so far as the relative rates of yield on government securities and other assets place the individual in a more preferred position.

This demonstration that the De Viti argument does not show that public debt should not be repaid cannot be applied in reverse. By saying that De Viti De Marco was wrong in making this extension is not to say that public debt *should be repaid.*

Puviani and the Fiscal Illusion

The contributions discussed so far have for the most part been due to the "economic" branch of Italian fiscal theory represented notably by De Viti De Marco and Einaudi. Several of the particular contributions are derivative from the general methodological approach, which recognizes the productivity of public services. The opposing school of thought has also made useful contributions, and, in some respects, these are more original and unique. Therefore, in some criteria, they should assume first rank. By far the most important of these is the idea of the fiscal illusion. It does not come directly from orthodox Italian fiscal theory, for it has scarcely been noted to a greater degree in Italy than elsewhere. The idea, vaguely expressed in the works of many writers, earlier and later, was crystallized in the work of one man, Amilcare Puviani, who wrote around the turn of the century.[35] In his time, his efforts were largely ignored, and it is only after his "rediscovery" by Fasiani that his ideas have now begun to exert some considerable influence on Italian thought.[36] Almost simultaneously, other continental writers are beginning to incorporate essentially similar ideas into their works on fiscal theory, although apparently independently of the ideas of Puviani.[37]

Puviani was, above all else, a political realist. He looked at the world around him and saw no sign of genuine democratic participation in the process of making collective choices. Such choices appeared to him to be made by the ruling or governing class, and he entertained no illusions about these choices being made in accordance with any vague criteria of general interest. The choices were not even conceived to be rationally made for the benefit of the governing class itself. Decisions as such were usually made on pragmatic grounds, and each was reached on the basis of causing the minimum of social friction.

From this approach Puviani constructed his hypothesis. He stated that the actions of the government could best be explained by the hypothesis that the government always acts to hide the burden of taxes from the public and to magnify the benefits of public expenditures. He was careful to state that governments do not actually do this as a deliberate plan. His hypothesis is, like all such similar ones, advanced as a working model, an *as if* sort of theoretical structure. When the governing group is successful in these attempts, fiscal illusions are created which effectively modify human behavior.

35. Puviani's main work is *Teoria della illusione finanziaria* (Palermo: 1903). This book, which was published in a limited edition, is now extremely difficult to locate, and I have not been able to consult it directly. I am grateful to the late Professor Benvenuto Griziotti of the University of Pavia for the use of his personal copy of a somewhat older and equally rare Puviani book, *Teoria della illusione nelle entrate pubbliche* (Perugia: 1897).

36. Fasiani has thoroughly discussed and summarized the Puviani contribution in his treatise, and he includes direct quotations of the most important parts. See, Mauro Fasiani, *Principii di scienza delle finanze,* 2nd ed. (Turin: 1951), I, 78-188. I should also mention the work of Vinci, written on the occasion of the fiftieth anniversary of the appearance of Puviani's main volume. See, Felice Vinci, *La teoria dell' illusione finanziaria di A. Puviani nel suo cinquantesimo anniversario* (Milan: 1953).

37. Cf. P. L. Reynaud, "La psychologie du contribuable devant l'impôt," *Revue de Science et Legislation Financiere,* XXXIX (1947) and XL (1948).

How do the separate parts of the modern fiscal structure fit the Puviani hypothesis? We may look first of all at the revenue or tax side. There is first the effort of governments to secure as much revenue as possible through the use of the public domain, that is, income-producing property owned by the state. In so far as revenue can be raised from this source, private individuals do not consider themselves to undergo a net burden; the opportunity costs are not individualized, and no checks are imposed on government spending. The second and perhaps most obvious means of creating a fiscal illusion lies in the use of indirect taxes rather than direct taxes. The taxpayer-consumer is not able to isolate the public from the private part of his ordinary purchase price, and in this way the real value of his tax burden appears less than it might actually be. A third and equally evident means is provided in the raising of revenues through inflation of the monetary unit. Here the public clearly is hoodwinked, and it has been through the ages.

The remaining devices which governments use to create fiscal illusions are perhaps somewhat more subtle. Puviani said that the individual was not able to balance properly future income against current income. He will, therefore, consider the annual tax in perpetuity to be of less burden to him than the current capitalized value of that tax stream. Governments fully recognize this and, as a result, public loans are always favored for extraordinary expenditures in preference to extraordinary taxes or capital levies.

Governments also recognize that taxes are more accepted by the tax-paying public if the moment of payment is associated with some pleasurable, and preferably unusual, event. Herein lies the explanation of gift taxation, according to Puviani, and, in fact, all taxes on transfers of wealth. The case of taxation of lottery winnings is clear. Similarly, taxes on non-ordinary consumption expenditures which are representative of the fulfillment of life-long desires are explained on this basis. Examples are taxes on the purchase of fine jewels, objects of art, etc.

A device which always works, and which rings loud bells in application to fiscal structures today, is that of introducing taxes under the guise that they are temporary or expedient and then allowing them to become permanent fixtures of the system. Closely allied to this of course is the adage that the old tax is the good tax. This is a principle perfectly in accord with the basic Puviani hypothesis. The governing group will clearly consider the old tax as a good one because people have become accustomed to paying it, and, therefore, its payment does not create as much social disturbance as would a newly imposed tax of like amount.

Still another source of exploitation for the government is provided in the social conflict among classes. By playing off one class against the other, the government can secure the ready acceptance of taxes which would otherwise be difficult. As an example, Puviani states that the wealthy classes can be made to accept heavy taxes if the specter of the upheaval of the lower classes is presented to them. Or, if political and social forces should temporarily place one social class in great disfavor with the rest of the population, the government can take this opportunity to impose excessively heavy taxes upon the oppressed class or group.

Yet another Puviani example which strikes hard to the modern reader is the device of governments' posing the awful and dire consequences of the alternative to a proposed tax. Puviani says that the alternative of the destruction of the social system, the breakdown of international relations, etc. will habitually be posed when a new tax bill is proposed. Modern expenditures for national defense and for foreign aid are clear examples of this sort of attempt on the part of governments, even in nominally democratic societies such as our own.

Both the timing and the form of the tax also can foster fiscal illusions. If collected in small amounts and distributed over time, the tax will always appear to be less burdensome than one which is concentrated in time. Similarly, the collection of a given amount under the guise of many small taxes may well seem to exert less fiscal pressure than the collection of a like amount under one consolidated tax bill.

A final form of fiscal illusion involved in the levy of taxes comes about in the uncertainty concerning the actual incidence of the tax. Governments will try not to levy taxes for which the incidence is known. The aim will rather be to introduce as much uncertainty as is possible thus keeping the individual in the dark concerning the actual amount of tax which he does pay in real terms.

The examples of fiscal illusions discussed above all appear on the revenue side and act so as to make the taxpayer think that he is paying less than he actually does pay toward the cost of government. The fiscal illusion can be equally important, and is equally used, on the expenditure side. Here the procedure is that of making the taxpayer think that he is getting more from public services than he actually does get. Puviani points out that the taxpayers, through their representatives, have always demanded the right to approve taxes independently and in advance of the demand for the right to make appropriations. And, even where the right of making appropriations has been won from executive authorities, the specialization of modern budgets prevents genuine control from being exercised. This provides the executive authority, the government, with an excellent opportunity to use fiscal illusions in the securing of legislative approval. For this reason, the executive tries to keep the budget as complex as is possible,[38] while fostering the belief among the taxpayers that they are participating effectively in the control of spending.

Although it is not stressed by Puviani perhaps the most effective means through which the modern executive authority can distort public thinking concerning the efficacy of public expenditure lies in the use of generalized categories which are largely meaningless to the voter-taxpayer. In recent years in this country, almost all types of expenditure have been justified by the catch-all category "national defense" and active attempts have been made by the bureaucracy to render this budget category sacrosanct. If this goal could, in fact, be achieved, the fiscal illusion would be complete, and the executive authority would have effectively removed all public constraint. So long as the debate can be kept in terms of Air Force "Wings" without consideration of the make-up of

38. Although this is not the place for an extended discussion, the impact of the Puviani analysis on the very core of modern budgetary theory is evident. Budgetary theory has been formulated on the implicit assumption that some omniscient executive acts genuinely in the "public interest." Once the ruling class conception of the executive is raised or admitted, the whole budgetary conception must, of course, be drastically modified.

such categories, the illusion will remain. The Puviani approach suggests, of course, that the most productive of all legislative activity in this age of budget specialization is precisely that of the much-ridiculed investigation into the "paper clips for the Navy." Only by the potential threat of detailed examination of budgetary items, can the normal executive power be kept within reasonable bounds.

The importance of the Puviani-Fasiani idea of the fiscal illusion does not lie in any of the particular examples from modern fiscal practice which it does seem to explain. Its importance is rather to be found in the fact that such a large proportion of the modern fiscal system can be explained by a hypothesis which is directly contrary either to the De Viti-Einaudi conception of the public economy or to the classical Anglo-Saxon conception of a fiscal structure based on "ability-to-pay." Puviani asked two simple questions: (1) If a completely rational dictator or class desires to exploit the taxpaying public to the greatest possible degree, what sort of fiscal system will result? (2) To what extent do modern fiscal systems approach this model? As the above discussion indicates, the fit is a surprisingly good one, and certainly the Puviani hypothesis must take its place among the important contributions to fiscal theory. As Fasiani pointed out, this hypothesis does not serve as the single explanation, but neither does any other.

Puviani made no attempt to extend his analysis toward the development of normative principles for fiscal activity. He was merely explaining what happens in the autocratic state. If, however, democratic ideals are accepted, Puviani's analysis points the way toward a set of norms for fiscal activity.[39]

The Coercive Element in Fiscal Choice

It is but natural that those theorists who locate effective decision-making power in a directing class or group should also

39. It is along these lines that I hope to do considerably more work. A whole set of fiscal principles can be developed on the presumption that fiscal choice should result from individual behavior which is as rational as is possible. Therefore, as a normative proposition, all fiscal illusions must be removed. On this basis, important criticism can be made against many elements of the existing fiscal structure.

have emphasized the coercive elements which are involved in the fiscal process. In so doing they have been able to provide both an incisive critique of the "economic" or voluntary theories of collective choice and a substantial contribution in their own right. Important figures in this tradition are Conigliani, Montemartini, Barone, Murray, and Cosciani.

These writers attempt to construct an economic theory of public finance along with those like De Viti and Einaudi and opposed to those like Pareto and Borgatta who deny this as a possibility. But while the economic aspects of fiscal choice are central to this approach, the location of the choice-making power is no longer with the individual, who is both producer and consumer of the public services. The fiscal decisions are made by some directing or ruling class which is, by definition or implication, smaller than the total group. Once this is accepted as a premise, it is evident that fiscal decisions can only be carried out through coercion. It would be unreasonable to expect that individuals who do not participate in the choice process should voluntarily accept and comply with such decisions as may be made.

Montemartini is the apparent source of many of the ideas in this tradition, and his ideas are especially interesting.[40] He viewed the state as an enterprise which produces the service of coercion; the political entrepreneurs purchase this service in order to carry out economic aims. Such political entrepreneurs have available to them three means of meeting any given objective. They may, first of all, achieve it by individual action. Secondly, they may form a voluntary and private association and undertake cooperative action. Thirdly, they may ask that the state do it for them. In choosing among these alternatives, this group will be guided by least-cost criteria. If, by purchasing coercion from the state, the group is able to reduce its own cost, it will choose this means. But Montemartini was clear in his emphasis that the service of coercion itself was costly.

His numerical example is perhaps worth repeating. Suppose that we are considering a society of ten individuals with equal incomes of $10 each. Now suppose that eight of these desire that

40. G. Montemartini, "Le base fondamentali di una scienza finanziaria pura," *Giornale degli economisti* (1900), II, 555-76.

$56 be spent collectively for the provision of a public water supply. The other two desire that water be provided through individual private efforts. If the eight form a voluntary cooperative association, the cost to each will be $7. But if they can secure the service through a community effort which is financed by a general tax, this cost will be reduced to $5.60. From this example, Montemartini indicated that the lower cost criteria may not always be relevant to the choosing of a collective action over a private one. But the example is not yet complete. The cost of imposing the necessary coercion on the two reluctant individuals has not been taken into account. And if these are fully considered, the public administration of the service may not be selected, even if the actual outlay necessary to finance the service is reduced by public action. Suppose that the public activity can reduce the cost from $56 to $50. If the costs of coercing the two minority members should be greater than $20, the majority of eight would still find it to their advantage to form the private association.

The Montemartini analysis clearly points up one of the major shortcomings of the De Viti-Einaudi analysis if the latter is considered to be explanatory rather than normative. This is the implication that the state's usage of the resources taken away from private employments by taxes must be at least as productive as private uses from which these resources are withdrawn. Unless unanimity is present in the choice (a point which Wicksell clearly perceived and upon which he based his tax theory) there is no assurance that, even in so-called democratic choice processes, the real income of the community will be increased by the allocation of income to public uses.

The essential thesis of several writers in this tradition, notably Conigliani, Murray and Barone,[41] is that collective choices are by their nature different from individual choices. The basis for this argument is the distinction which was made by both Pantaleoni and Pareto between the problem of maximizing individual welfare and maximizing collective or social welfare. Pantaleoni argued

41. See, C. A. Conigliani, "L'indirizzo teorico nella scienza finanziaria," *Giornale degli economisti* (1894), II, 105-29; R. A. Murray, "I problemi fondamentali dell' economia finanziaria," *Giornale degli economisti* (1912), I, 255-301; E. Barone, *Le opere economiche, Vol. III, Principi di economia finanziaria* (Bologna: 1937).

that collective action need not imply coercion so long as it was aimed at the satisfaction of individual utilities. In this case individuals would freely and voluntarily contribute the necessary revenues to finance the public services.[42] In the terminology of modern welfare economics, this would indicate that some collective action could be carried out in accordance with the Paretian criteria for increasing general welfare. Conigliani, Murray, and the others were quick to point out, however, that this sort of action need not involve the state at all. If people will voluntarily contribute to finance state services, anarchism is the ideal social system. They argued that the very need for the state arose only because this was not the typical situation and that coercion was the one essential characteristic of all state action. Pantaleoni admitted the necessity of coercion when the state attempts to maximize in any way collective or social welfare. And he made a distinction between the maximization of individual welfare and the maximization of social welfare even within the choice pattern of the individual. This suggests that each individual acts in accordance with an individualized or personal-utility or preference scale and at the same time with a social preference scale. These may come into conflict at many points, and the individual may deliberately choose to be coerced and to coerce others if the social preference scale is overruling.

Pareto's distinction between the achievement of maximum utility *of* the society and the achievement of the maximum utility *for* the society is similar to that of Pantaleoni.[43] Murray, a close follower of Pareto, extended the Pareto analysis to the problem of fiscal choice. He tried to show that the achievement of any sort of collective or social maximum is impossible without the violation of some of the necessary conditions for the attainment of the individual maxima. State action necessarily implies some attempt in this direction; therefore, coercion is necessary.

Barone's conception of state activity was similar although somewhat more clearly stated. He pointed up the weakness in the

42. M. Pantaleoni, "Cenni sul concetto di massimi edonistici individuali e collettivi," *Giornale degli economisti* (1891), and reprinted in *Scritti varii di economia* (Rome: 1904), pp. 281-340.

43. V. Pareto, "Il massimo di utilità per una collettivita in Sociologia," *Giornale degli economisti* (1913), I, 336-341.

voluntary theory of fiscal choice by showing that it is impossible to fix some distribution of the tax burden among individuals and then to say that the amount of public services is chosen voluntarily. The prefixing of the distribution of the tax burden, which is implicit in the work of De Viti and Einaudi, is essentially equivalent to choosing a social welfare function. Once this is chosen and action taken in accordance with it, no pretense of voluntary choice can be maintained. Coercion must be introduced. The individual is not allowed to calculate the utility of public services and make his contributive choice accordingly. Barone sensed fully the necessity of the requirement of a Wicksellian unanimity in order to justify the use of any sort of voluntary theory of fiscal choice. But he denied the possibility of such unanimity being attained; therefore, the theory of finance reduces to the theory of the coercive distribution of the tax burden.

Cosciani is the modern interpreter of this tradition in Italian fiscal theory.[44] He states that the study of finance consists in the examination of the reasons for and the effects of the substitution of coercive collective choices for individual choices. Two sets of individual behavior are involved; first, that of the ruling class in making the decisions, and secondly, that of the taxpaying group in responding to the alternatives put before them. Anglo-Saxon fiscal theory has, of course, almost exclusively been concentrated on the second of these two sets of behavior. In a very real sense, therefore, our theoretical structure is more in keeping with the ruling-class tradition than with the voluntary tradition. The merit of the ruling-class conception appears to be its usefulness in forcing the separate consideration of these two aspects of fiscal action.

Miscellaneous Contributions

Italian theorists have made several other, and more specific, contributions. A few of these may be noted briefly. The first consists in the application of the Paretian indifference curve apparatus to the classical problem of the relative burden of the income tax and the consumption tax. This application was first made by Barone in 1912, utilized again by Borgatta in 1921, and further

44. C. Cosciani, *Principii di scienza della finanze* (Turin: 1953).

developed by Fasiani in 1930.[45] It did not appear in English until the celebrated note by Miss Joseph was published in 1939.[46] This "excess burden" analysis has recently been criticized, and correctly so, on the basis of the attempts which have been made to extend the conclusions reached to any general statements relative to the merits of the general income tax and the excise tax. It is interesting to note, however, that this extension was not made by Barone or Fasiani. Both emphasized the partial-equilibrium nature of the conclusions reached and specifically warned that the analysis could not easily be applied to the community as a whole.

A second contribution closely related to the same analysis is that made by Gobbi. He argued that there is no difference in the burden of a consumption tax and an income tax of equal yield.[47] This was based on the alleged invalidity of the Marshallian concept of consumers' surplus. It seems clear that Gobbi was thinking in terms of the community as a whole, and that his rejection of consumers' surplus is based on an early recognition that this is not additive and, therefore, it is of little use in general tax analysis. He stated that the consumer's surplus for all goods must be zero.[48]

A third contribution, made by Pareto and developed to some extent by Borgatta, consists in nothing more than some fragmentary ideas which seem to offer some insights into the process of fiscal choice. Clearly recognizing that all actual choices must be made by individuals, whether in their capacity as taxpayer-voters or as members of some ruling class, Pareto argued that the individual choices which go into the making of collective decisions are necessarily non-logical. It is therefore erroneous to attribute rationality to such choices and to judge them by any criteria of rational behavior. Non-logical action is not equivalent to purposefully

45. E. Barone, "Studi di economia finanziaria," *Giornale degli economisti* (1912), II, 329-30 in notes; G. Borgatta, "Intorno alla pressione di qualunque imposta a parità di prelievo," *Giornale degli economisti* (1921), II, 290-97; M. Fasiani, "Di un particolare aspetto delle imposte sul consumo," *La riforma sociale,* XL (1930), 1-20.

46. M. F. W. Joseph, "The Excess Burden of Indirect Taxation," *Review of Economic Studies,* VI (1938-1939), 226-31.

47. U. Gobbi, "Un preteso difetto delle imposte sui consumi," *Giornale degli economisti* (1904), I, 296-306.

48. *Ibid.,* p. 301.

irrational action. Rather it is action which may be ruled by mixed motives, which has no fixed objective, which involves many uncertainties. The chooser is not able to predict the results of his behavior with any degree of certainty, and even if he could do so, he would have little idea as to what goals he really seeks to maximize. Social man is essentially different from individual man. Out of the complex of actions which are taken, some logical, some non-logical, it may be possible to discover some uniformities and it is here that a theory of finance must be discovered. It is not surprising that these ideas were not carried much further than this,[49] but any theory of collective choice must take the Paretian conception into account. It suffices to throw out both the voluntaristic approach, which assumes the taxpayer-voter to act similarly to his action in the private economy, and the organismic approach, which attributes some superior rationality to the collective entity.

V. A COMPARATIVE SUMMARY

This discussion of the Italian tradition in fiscal theory may be concluded by a brief comparison with the Anglo-Saxon tradition. The latter is directly related to neo-classical economics and is specifically Marshallian in its essentials. Anglo-Saxon fiscal theory has analyzed the effects of particular fiscal measures (almost exclusively tax measures) upon the private economy. The analysis has normally been conceived in a partial-equilibrium framework, although recently the Keynesian influence has served to shift this emphasis somewhat. The usefulness of Anglo-Saxon thought depends upon, and is limited by, this characteristic feature. Fiscal theory has been an adjunct of economic theory, and as such, it has been useful for many purposes, but it has been little else.[50]

It is appropriate to ask whether this is the proper role for finance theory. Surely the function of such theorizing must be

49. See G. Borgatta, "Lo studio scientifico dei fenomeni finanziari," *Giornale degli economisti* (1920), I, 1-24, 81-116, for a good discussion of this point of view. For Pareto's own statement, see G. Sensini, *Corrispondenza di Vilfredo Pareto* (Padua: 1948), cited in M. Fasiani, "Contributi di Pareto alla scienza delle finanze," *Giornale degli economisti* (1949), p. 156.

50. This point is made by Earl Rolph, *The Theory of Fiscal Economics* (Berkeley: University of California Press, 1954), p. ix.

that of analyzing and explaining the results of government action, however this action may be motivated. But government is co-dimensional with the whole economy and includes within its scope all of the individual units of this economy. Government action cannot, therefore, be limited in any genuine sense to any specific subsector. As Del Vecchio wisely remarks, it is impossible properly to conceive fiscal theory in other than general-equilibrium terms. This does not suggest the necessity of using Walrasian-Paretian models for all fiscal problems, but it does imply that the interdependence among variables must be fully recognized. Spill-over effects cannot simply be neglected in the faith that these will fade away and become unimportant as is the case in so many areas of applied economics. By their very nature fiscal problems are general welfare problems, not the problems of particular groups of persons, classes, or industries.

The great merit of the Italians is that they have placed fiscal theory in a broad framework in which the necessary interdependence has been fully recognized. By and large, their system is internally consistent. The weaknesses are much the same as those of Walrasian economics. Problem-solving has been relatively neglected. We find, for example, little discussion of the incidence of particular taxes or expenditures. But we should not measure contributions in terms of wordage on either side. A great deal of the Anglo-Saxon discussion on incidence has been of little value precisely because the general-equilibrium aspects of the problems have not been taken into account.

Contemporary Italian economists will freely admit that their tradition has suffered from an excess of "system" at the expense of "problem-solving." But all good Marshallians must acknowledge just as freely that the latter effort is fruitful only in so far as the "system" or the methodology is sound. While Fubini was correct in holding Marshall up as an idol to the Italian theorists, perhaps a good dose of Ferrara would be equally helpful to modern fiscal Marshallians.

The English-language tradition has almost completely neglected the second major problem of fiscal theory, that of collective choice. This has been introduced only in welfare economics, and this sometimes-rarified branch of study has rarely been tied to fiscal theory.[51] The Italian emphasis upon the state or the public entity as the subject of analysis, rather than the private economy, has forced attention to the problem of choice, in reference both to the collective unit and to the individual taxpayer-beneficiary. Much remains to be accomplished here, but students must look to the Italian and other continental sources, notably Wicksell, for any hints and directions; the Anglo-Saxons have defaulted, with the very recent exceptions noted above.

Finally, no reforming spirit has guided the Italians. This has made their arguments seem sterile and devoid of normative content. The normative elements which are present are usually clouded over, perhaps unintentionally, with pseudo-scientific pronouncements. This has not been a strong feature of the Italian tradition, but we can lay little claim to superiority here. Unconsciously trapped by our utilitarian heritage, we have accepted and promoted all of the nonsense which is contained in the theories of proportional, equal, and minimum sacrifice, etc. Only a handful of writers, such as Henry Simons, have been able to break through the enveloping fog.

Italian fiscal theory has many deficiencies, and it is certainly not lacking in its own varieties of nonsense. This "science" seems peculiarly addicted to the attraction of "fuzziness," whatever the land of origin. It may perhaps be charged that precious time is wasted in the attempt to sift old and foreign doctrines for good ideas. But if any progress is to be made, fiscal theory must break out of its current strait-jacket, and a hybridization may be required to accomplish this. Economists simply cannot neglect a fundamental re-examination of the whole orthodoxy upon which economic policy in this most important subject area has been, and continues to be, made.

Bibliographical Note

The student interested in a short history of the Italian work in fiscal theory should look first at G. Del Vecchio, *Introduzione alla*

51. The recent efforts by Bowen, Musgrave, and Samuelson provide notable exceptions.

finanza, 2nd ed. (Padua: 1957). A summary history of doctrine may also be found in L. Gangemi, *Elementi di scienza delle finanze* (Naples: 1948). For a single article summarizing the Italian contribution, Borgatta's introduction to the Italian translation of Wicksell's *Finanztheoretische Untersuchungen* and other essays is recommended (*Nuova Collana di Economisti,* Vol. IX, *Finanza* [Turin: 1934]).

The student interested in going to the original source for a surprisingly large proportion of the Italian ideas is directed to the work of Ferrara. Of all the Italians, Pareto included, Ferrara must assume first rank, and in his work may be found germs of later developments, not only in fiscal theory, but in all of economic theory as well. His complete works are only now in the process of being issued, volumes I, II, III and IV having been published (Francesco Ferrara, *Opere complete* [Rome: 1955, 1956]). His work in fiscal theory is largely contained in his lectures, which were taken as notes (Ferrara, *Lezioni di economia politica,* 2 vols., [Bologna: 1934]).

Pantaleoni's works in public finance are scattered and they have not been collected in a single volume. Barone's major writings on finance are available in Volume III of his works (Enrico Barone, *Le opere economiche,* Vol. III, *Principi di economia finanziaria* [Bologna: 1937]). The English translation of De Viti De Marco's *First Principles of Public Finance* is available, but this book does not, in itself, properly convey the Italian contribution. Einaudi's treatise is recommended: Luigi Einaudi, *Principii di scienza della finanza,* 3rd ed. (Turin: 1945), but his best work has appeared in his essays; the most important collection of his essays is *Saggi sul risparmio e l'imposta* (Turin: 1941).

Almost all of the important work appeared in the professional journals prior to its later publication in book form. Prior to 1920, the *Giornale degli economisti* contained almost all of the important papers. After about 1920, Einaudi's review, *La riforma sociale* began to attract important contributions.

At the present time, the most important Italian journal in public finance is *Rivista di diritto finanziario e scienza delle finanze,* which was founded by the late Professor Griziotti and which is issued at the University of Pavia.

The most important single work which appeared in Italy in the postwar period has been the second edition of the late Mauro Fasiani's treatise, *Principii di scienza delle finanze,* 2 vols. (Turin: 1951).

III

SOCIAL CHOICE, DEMOCRACY, AND FREE MARKETS*

PROFESSOR Kenneth Arrow's provocative essay, *Social Choice and Individual Values,*[1] has stimulated a great deal of comment and discussion since its publication. Reviewers and discussants have been primarily concerned with those formal aspects of Arrow's analysis which relate to modern welfare economics. This concentration, which is explained by both the stated purpose of the work and the tools with which it is developed, has resulted in the neglect of the broader philosophical implications of the essay.[2] In this paper I propose to examine the arguments of Arrow and his critics within a more inclusive frame of reference. This approach reveals a weakness in the formal analysis itself and demonstrates that some of the more significant implications drawn from the analysis are inappropriate.

I shall first review briefly Arrow's argument, in order to isolate the source of much of the confusion which has been generated by it. Following this, I shall raise some questions concerning the philosophical basis of the concept of social rationality. In the

* Reprinted without significant change from the *Journal of Political Economy,* LXII (1954), 114-23. I am indebted to Marshall Colberg, Jerome Milliman, and Proctor Thompson, for helpful comments and suggestions.

1. New York: John Wiley & Sons, 1951.

2. Little's stimulating review article and, to a somewhat lesser extent, Rothenberg's subsequent critique provide partial exceptions to this general statement (see I. M. D. Little, "Social Choice and Individual Values," *Journal of Political Economy,* LX [1952], 422-32; and Jerome Rothenberg, "Conditions for a Social Welfare Function," *Journal of Political Economy,* LXI [1953], 389-405).

next section I shall attempt to show that the negative results of Arrow's analysis as applied to voting represent established and desirable features of the decision-making process embodied in constitutional democracy. From this it follows that if the conditions required by Arrow were satisfied, certain modifications in the underlying institutional structure would become imperative. Finally, I shall develop the argument that the voting process is fundamentally different from the market when the two are considered as decision-making processes rather than as bases for deriving social welfare functions. Here it will be demonstrated that the market does produce consistent choices and that the market does not belong in the category of collective choice at all.

I. ARROW'S CONDITIONS FOR THE SOCIAL WELFARE FUNCTION

Arrow first defines his problem as that of constructing an ordering relation for society as a whole which will also reflect rational choice-making. This construction requires the establishment of a weak ordering relation among alternative social states. He then defines the social welfare function as a "*process* or rule which, for each set of individual orderings . . . *states* a corresponding social ordering" (italics mine).[3] The language is extremely important here, and the use of the word "process" seems singularly unfortunate. This usage has apparently been the source of the confusion, which is present in both the original essay and most of the criticism, between the definition of the social welfare function and the actual *processes* of choice: voting and the market. As will be shown in this paper, the decision-making *process* may produce consistent choice, even though the *rule* which *states* the social ordering from the individual values may not exist.

Having defined the social welfare function, Arrow proceeds to set up the conditions which are necessary to insure that it will be based on individual values. These conditions have received the bulk of attention in the discussion of Arrow's work and are so generally familiar that they may be merely listed here. They include the requirements that (1) the function shall not be im-

3. Arrow, *op. cit.,* p. 23.

posed; (2) it shall not be dictated by any one individual; (3) if one individual prefers one social alternative to another and everyone else is indifferent between the two, the preferred alternative shall not stand lower in the social ordering; and (4) irrelevant social alternatives shall not affect the ranking of relevant alternatives.[4]

Having set up these necessary conditions, Arrow develops his General Possibility Theorem (p. 59) which states that, if there are at least three alternatives, every social welfare function satisfying the rationality conditions along with requirements 3 and 4 above must violate the condition either of non-imposition or of non-dictatorship. The theorem is proved to be applicable to the method of majority decision as a *welfare function* and to the market as a *welfare function.* It is inapplicable only when there exists unanimous agreement among all individuals concerning alternative social states, when the required majority of individuals possess identical orderings of social alternatives, or when individual orderings are characterized as "single-peaked." Since each of these possibilities appears somewhat remote, the weight of Arrow's argument is to the effect that the individual values which are implicit in the normal decision-making mechanisms of society do not provide methods of deriving social welfare functions that are neither imposed nor dictatorial. So far, so good. But Arrow extends the argument to say that these ordinary decision-making mechanisms do not allow rational social choice.[5] Now this is a horse of quite a different color, with which the Arrow argument should not legitimately concern itself at all. Arrow is not at all clear as to which of these two animals he is chasing. The title of his essay implies that he is concerned with decision-making processes, and he begins his work by reference to the democratic means of decision-making—voting and the market. He states his General Possibility Theorem in terms of "moving from individual tastes to social *preferences*" (italics mine).[6] Yet he slips almost imperceptibly into the terminology of social-ordering rela-

4. For the most concise listing of these conditions see William Baumol's review in *Econometrica,* XX (1952), 110.
5. *Op. cit.,* p. 59.
6. *Ibid.*

tions or social welfare functions when he sets up his required conditions. He fails to see that his conditions, *properly interpreted, apply only to the derivation of the function and do not apply directly to the choice processes.*[7] As will be shown in Section III below, this distinction is not important in application to voting, and this appears to be the root of some of the difficulty. As will be shown in Section IV, when the market is considered, this distinction is fundamental. It will be proved that the existence of an Arrow social welfare function is not a necessary condition for consistent decision-making.

Unfortuately, but understandably, the Arrow argument has been widely interpreted in the erroneous sense of proving that the decision-making processes are irrational or inconsistent.[8] To the critics and reviewers of his analysis, almost without exception, Arrow appears to have subjected voting and the market to the test for rationality and to have found both these processes wanting.

II. THE CONCEPT OF SOCIAL RATIONALITY

It is difficult to know exactly what is meant by "rational social choice" in the Arrow analysis. Social rationality appears to imply that the choice-making processes produce results which are indicated to be "rational" by the ordering relation, that is, the social welfare function. But why should this sort of social rationality be expected? Certainly not because it is required for the derivation of the function in the first place. The mere introduction of the idea of social rationality suggests the fundamental philosophical issues involved. Rationality or irrationality as an attribute

7. Little objects to Arrow's failure to draw a distinction between the social welfare function and decision-making process on quite different grounds from those advanced here. His objections are primarily centered on Arrow's labeling the ordering as a "social welfare function" rather than merely as the resultant of the decision-making process (Little, *op. cit.,* pp. 427-30). He thus fails, along with Arrow, to make the necessary distinction between an ordering of social states possessing certain properties and a decision-making process which is consistent, that is, rational.

Rothenberg, on the other hand, explicity defines the results of the choice process as the social welfare function (*op. cit.,* p. 400). He fails, however, to trace through the effects of this definition on the Arrow analysis.

8. See, e.g., J. C. Weldon, "On the Problem of Social Welfare Functions," *Canadian Journal of Economics and Political Science,* XVIII (1952), 452-64.

of the social group implies the imputation to that group of an organic existence apart from that of its individual components. If the social group is so considered, questions may be raised relative to the wisdom or unwisdom of this organic being. But does not the very attempt to examine such rationality in terms of individual values introduce logical inconsistency at the outset? Can the rationality of the social organism be evaluated in accordance with any value ordering other than its own?

The whole problem seems best considered as one of the "either-or" variety. We may adopt the philosophical bases of individualism in which the individual is the only entity possessing ends or values. In this case no question of social or collective rationality may be raised. A social value scale as such simply does not exist. Alternatively, we may adopt some variant of the organic philosophical assumptions in which the collectivity is an independent entity possessing its own value ordering. It is legitimate to test the rationality or irrationality of this entity only against this value ordering.[9]

The usefulness of either of these opposing philosophical foundations may depend upon the type of problems to be faced.[10] But the two should always be sharply distinguished, and it should be made clear that any social value scale may be discussed only within an organic framework. Once this approach is taken, the question as to whether or not the social value scale may be based on individual values may properly be raised,[11] and the individual orderings of all possible social states may be the appropriate starting point in the construction of a social ordering that is to be

9. By his statement that "every value judgment must be someone's judgment of values" (*op. cit.*, p. 427), Little appears fully to accept what I have called the "individualistic assumptions" and, in doing so, to deny the possible existence of an organic social unit. In his critique Rothenberg seems to adhere to the organic conception, when he states that "social valuation as opposed to solely individual valuation is an existential reality" (*op. cit.*, p. 397).

10. The point involved here is closely related to a central problem in the pure theory of government finance. The whole body of doctrine in this field has suffered from the failure of theorists to separate the two approaches ("The Pure Theory of Government Finance: A Suggested Approach," *supra*, Essay I, Sections II and III).

11. Whether or not the degree of dependence on individual values is or is not a good criterion of appropriateness for a social ordering depends, in turn, on one's own value scale. We may or may not agree with Rothenberg when he says that consensus is required for a good social welfare function (*op. cit.*, p. 398).

based on individual values. But the appropriateness of such individual orderings for this purpose does not depend on the fact that these are sufficient to allow the ordinary decision-making processes to function.

Voting and the market, as decision-making mechanisms, have evolved from, and are based upon an acceptance of, the philosophy of individualism which presumes no social entity. These processes are related only indirectly to the individual values entering into any welfare function. This was true even in the pre-Robbins state of welfare economics. The measurability and comparability of utility did provide a means by which individual psychological attributes could be amalgamated into a conceptual social magnitude. The social welfare function of the utilitarians was based, in this way, on components imputable to individuals. But the welfare edifice so constructed was not necessarily coincident with that resulting from the ordinary choice-making processes. It was made to appear so because the utilitarians were also individualists[12] and, in one sense, philosophically inconsistent.

Arrow's work, correctly interpreted, consists in rigorously proving that the individual orderings of alternatives which are sufficient to allow the decision-making processes to function produce no such measuring stick as was provided by the measurability of utility. The overthrow of such measurability destroyed the conceptual social welfare function; there are no longer any units of account.[13] Arrow's analysis *appears* to consist, however, in proving that the decision-making processes themselves define no social welfare function, that is, do not produce rational social choice. And here the implication is strong that this is true only when an ordinal concept of utility is substituted for a cardinal concept.

12. Cf. Lionel Robbins, *The Theory of Economic Policy in English Classical Political Economy* (London: Macmillan & Co., Ltd., 1952), p. 182.

13. Several of the attempts to modify Arrow's conditions in such a way as to define an acceptable social welfare function involve, in one form or another, a revival of the interpersonal comparability of utility (see Murray Kemp and A. Asimakopulos, "A Note on Social Welfare Functions and Cardinal Utility," *Canadian Journal of Economics and Political Science,* XVIII [1952], 195-200; Leo Goodman and Harry Markowitz, "Social Welfare Functions Based on Individual Rankings," *American Journal of Sociology,* LVIII [1952], 257-62; Clifford Hildreth, "Alternative Conditions for Social Orderings," *Econometrica,* XXI [1953], 81-95).

Actually, the decision-making processes do not produce "rational" social choice, even in the utilitarian framework, until and unless certain restrictive assumptions are made.

If social rationality is defined as producing results indicated as rational by the welfare function, that is, maximizing total utility in the utilitarian framework, a market decision is socially rational only if individuals are rational and individual utilities are independent. A voting decision is socially rational only if individual voting power is somehow made proportional to individual utility. Cardinal utility allowed the economist to construct a social welfare function from the individual utilities; it did nothing to insure that market or voting choices were socially rational. Here the distinction between a rational choice process and an acceptable social welfare function becomes evident.

The proper approach to social welfare functions appears to begin with the frank admission that such functions are social, not individual, and therefore are of a fundamentally different philosophical dimension than individual values in individualistically-oriented decision-making processes. It seems meaningless to attempt to test such choice processes for social "rationality." But if the idea of acceptable social welfare functions and of social or collective rationality is completely divorced from the decision-making processes of the group, what is there left of the Arrow analysis? It is still possible to test these processes for consistency,[14] but consistency or rationality in this sense must not be defined in terms of results obtainable from a social ordering. Consistency must be defined in terms of satisfying "the condition of rationality, as we ordinarily understand it."[15] This implies only that choices can be made (are connected) and that the choices are transitive. The implications of the Arrow argument appear to be that such consistency of choice, could it be achieved, would be a highly desirable feature of decision-making. I shall attempt in the following section to show that possible inconsistency of collective choice as applied to voting is a necessary and highly useful characteristic of political democracy.

14. Cf. Little, *op. cit.,* p. 432.
15. Arrow, *op. cit.,* p. 3.

III. MAJORITY DECISION AND COLLECTIVE CHOICE

The reaching of decisions by majority vote provides one of the simplest voting rules. In the historical and philosophical context, majority decisions evolved as a means through which a social group makes collective choices among alternatives when consensus among the individuals comprising the group cannot be attained. Correctly speaking, majority decision must be viewed primarily as a device for breaking a stalemate and for allowing some collective action to be taken. A decision reached through the approval of a majority with minority dissent has never been, and should never be, correctly interpreted as anything other than a provisional or experimental choice of the whole social group. As a tentative choice, the majority-determined policy is held to be preferred to inaction,[16] but it is not to be considered as irrevocable. The fact that such decisions may be formally inconsistent provides one of the most important safeguards against abuse through this form of the voting process.[17] If consistency were a required property of decision, majority rule would not prove acceptable, even as a means of reaching provisional choices at the margins of the social-decision surface.

One of the most important limitations placed upon the exercise of majority rule lies in the temporary nature of the majorities. One social alternative may be chosen during a legislative session, but a new and temporary majority may reverse the decision during the same or the next session. A majority may reject C in favor of B, and then select A over B, but still select C over A when put to yet another test. The obvious result of this so-called "paradox"

16. For a discussion of the basis for majority decision, see Robert A. Dahl and Charles E. Lindblom, *Politics, Economics, and Welfare* (New York: Harper & Bros., 1953), pp. 43 ff.

17. Throughout this section the term "inconsistency" will be used in the formal sense without specific reference to the question of time dimension. This is admissible if it is assumed that all individuals have sufficient knowledge of alternatives to enable each to rank all alternatives and if it is assumed further that neither these individual orderings nor the available alternatives change over time. These assumptions, which are central to the Arrow analysis, allow the time dimension of the voting paradox to be neglected. When knowledge of alternatives is not perfect, however, and when the individual orderings do change over time (cf. *infra*) or the alternatives presented vary, the concept of inconsistency itself becomes extremely vague. The argument of this section is applicable, however, whether or not the conditions required for the formal analysis are satisfied.

of voting is that the social group cannot make a firm and definite choice among the alternatives offered.[18] Thus the voting process does not necessarily produce consistency of choice, and, within the Arrow framework, the individual rankings required for voting cannot be translated by the economist into a satisfactory social welfare function. The implication is that both these results are undesirable; the transitivity property is not present.

But, certainly, majority rule is acceptable in a free society precisely because it allows a sort of jockeying back and forth among alternatives, upon none of which relative unanimity can be obtained. Majority rule encourages such shifting, and it provides the opportunity for any social decision to be altered or reversed at any time by a new and temporary majority grouping. In this way, majority decision-making itself becomes a means through which the whole group ultimately attains consensus, that is, makes a genuine social choice. It serves to insure that competing alternatives may be experimentally and provisionally adopted, tested, and replaced by new compromise alternatives approved by a majority group of ever-changing composition. This is democratic choice process, whatever may be the consequences for welfare economics and social welfare functions.

The paradox is removed, and majority rule produces consistent choices in the formal sense, if the individual components of a majority possess identical orderings of all social alternatives. If, for example, Joe and Jack both prefer A to B to C, and Tom prefers C to B to A, Joe and Jack can always outvote Tom and adopt A. The selection of A would represent definite and irreversible choice as long as the individual orderings remain unchanged. This is one of the situations in which Arrow's General Possibility Theorem would not hold; a social welfare function may be derived, and the implication appears to be that such a situation would prove a more desirable one than that in which

18. Dahl and Lindblom accept fully this interpretation of the paradox when discussing it in specific reference to Arrow's work. They also dismiss the logical difficulty involved in the paradox as "minor" and "not an empirical observation of a common difficulty." In this latter respect, they apparently fail to see that the potential intransitivity property of ordinary majority voting provides a means of removing one of the greatest of all difficulties in the structure of majority rule (*op. cit.*, pp. 422 ff.).

inconsistency is present. In one of the most revealing statements in his essay Arrow says: "Suppose it is assumed in advance that a majority of individuals will have the same ordering of social alternatives. . . . Then the method of majority decision will pick out the agreed-on ordering and make it the social ordering. Again all the . . . conditions will be satisfied. These results reinforce the suggestion . . . that like attitudes toward social alternatives are needed for the formation of social judgments."[19] The above statement also shows that Arrow is primarily interested in individual values as the units of account to be used in deriving social welfare functions. It is the collective rationality with which he is concerned; his approach includes no consideration of individual values as ends as well as means.

If one examines the choices made in this case of identical majority orderings, it becomes evident that collective rationality or consistency is secured here only at a cost of imposing a literal "tyranny of the majority." Minorities under such conditions could no longer accept majority decisions without revolt. If there should exist policy areas in which specific majority groupings possess identical orderings of social alternatives, it would become necessary to impose additional restraints upon the exercise of majority decision. This was one of the considerations which led Wicksell to advocate the adoption of the principle of unanimity in the approval of tax bills. He reasoned that in the imposition of taxes the given majority in power would tend to be too cohesive and would, therefore, be able permanently to impose its will on the minority.[20]

The form in which Arrow states his condition of non-dictatorship is closely related to the point discussed above. This condition, as applied to group decision, states that no one individual must dictate the choice without regard to the values of other individuals.[21] From the individual minority member's point of view, however, the acceptance of irrevocable majority decision is not different from the acceptance of irrevocable authoritarian decision. In either case the choice is dictated to the individual in question,

19. *Op. cit.*, p. 74.

20. Knut Wicksell, *Finanztheoretische Untersuchungen* (Jena: Gustav Fischer, 1896), p. 122.

21. Arrow, *op. cit.*, p. 30.

since his values are overruled in the decision-making. If one thinks in terms of individual values as ends, "dictated to" seems a more meaningful concept than "dictated by."

The reason that majority rule proves tolerably acceptable and individual authoritarian dictatorship lies not in the many versus the one. It is because ordinary majority decision is subject to reversal and change, while individual decision cannot readily be made so. With identical majority orderings, the majority would, of course, always choose the same leaders, and this advantage of majority rule would be lost. It is not evident that we should summarily reject the rule of one individual if we could be assured that ever so often a new dictator would be chosen by lot and that everyone's name would be in the lottery.

The attempt to examine the consistency of majority voting requires the assumption that individual values do not themselves change during the decision-making process. The vulnerability of this assumption in the general case has been shown by Schoeffler.[22] Individual values are, of course, constantly changing; so a post-decision ordering may be different from a pre-decision ordering. The assumption of constancy may, however, be useful in certain instances. For example, the assumption of given tastes in the decision-making represented by the market is essential for the development of a body of economic theory. But the extension of this assumption to apply to individual values in the voting process disregards one of the most important functions of voting itself.[23] The definition of democracy as "government by discussion" implies that individual values can and do change in the process of decision-making. Men must be free to choose, and they must maintain an open mind if the democratic mechanism is to work at all. If individual values in the Arrow sense of orderings of all social alternatives are unchanging, discussion becomes meaningless. And the discussion must be considered as encompassing more than the activity prior to the initial vote. The whole period of activity

22. Sidney Schoeffler, "Note on Modern Welfare Economics," *American Economic Review*, XLII (1952), 880-87.

23. The difference in the validity of the constancy assumption in these two situations is stressed by L. J. Richenburg in his review of Duncan Black and R. A. Nevins, *Committee Decisions with Complementary Valuation*, in *Economic Journal*, LXII (1952), 131.

during which temporary majority decisions are reached and reversed, and new compromises appear and are approved or overthrown, must be considered as one of genuine discussion.

In a very real sense collective choice cannot be considered as being reached by voting until relatively unanimous agreement is achieved. In so far as the attainment of such consensus is impossible, it is preferable that the actual choice processes display possible inconsistency rather than guaranteed consistency. The molding and solidifying of individual values into fixed ordering relations sufficient to make ordinary majority voting fit the Arrow conditions for consistency would mean the replacement of accepted democratic process by something clearly less desirable. The danger that such solidification will take place becomes more imminent as functional economic groups, subjecting members to considerable internal discipline, seek to institutionalize individual values.

The unanimity requirement need not imply that consistent choice can never be reached by voting. Relatively complete consensus is present in the social group on many major issues, and the securing of such consensus need not involve the concept of a Rousseau-like general will. As Arrow points out,[24] the unanimity required may be reached at several levels. There may exist relatively general support of the framework within which change shall be allowed to take place, that is, the constitution. This in itself insures that a genuine attempt will be made to attain consensus on controversial issues and, more importantly, to insure that the changes which are made are introduced in an orderly and nonrevolutionary manner. This relative consensus on procedure, however, will exist only so long as majorities on particular issues do not solidify; in other words, as long as ordinary decision-making may be formally inconsistent.

IV. COLLECTIVE CHOICE AND FREE MARKETS

In his discussion Arrow fails to make any distinction between voting and the market mechanism as decision-making processes, and he specifically defines both as "special cases of the more general category of collective social choice."[25] He is led to this conclusion

24. *Op. cit.*, pp. 90 ff.
25. *Ibid.*, p. 5.

because he is unable to define a satisfactory social welfare function from the individual orderings required for either process. In the consideration of voting, it is a relatively simple step to discard the social rationality or social welfare function implications and to utilize the Arrow conditions in testing the consistency of the choice process. When this is done, it is found that ordinary majority rule does not necessarily produce consistent choices. Thus the voting process serves neither as a basis for deriving a social welfare function in the Arrow sense nor as a means of producing consistent choices if tested by the Arrow conditions. When the market is considered, however, a different result arises when the process is tested for consistency of choice from that which is forthcoming when one seeks to derive a social welfare function. A necessary condition for deriving a social welfare function is that all possible social states be ordered *outside* or *external* to the decision-making process itself. What is necessary, in effect, is that the one erecting such a function be able to translate the individual values (which are presumably revealed to him) into social building blocks. If these values consist only of individual orderings of social states (which is all that is required for either political voting or market choice), this step cannot be taken. This step in the construction of a social welfare function is the focal point in the Arrow analysis. This is clearly revealed in the statement: "The relation of known preference or indifference is clearly transitive, but it is not connected since, for example, *it does not tell us* how the individual compares two social alternatives, one of which yields him more of one commodity than the second, while the second yields him more of a second commodity than the first" (italics mine).[26]

By the very nature of free markets, however, the only entity required to compare two social alternatives when a choice is actually made is the individual. And, since individual orderings are assumed to be connected and transitive,[27] the market mechanism does provide a means of *making consistent choices* as long as individual values remain unchanged. If, given the constancy in individual tastes (values), the economic environment is allowed

26. Arrow, *op. cit.*, p. 61.
27. *Ibid.*, p. 34.

to change, consistency requires only that the same social state would always result from similar environmental changes. Of course, there is no way of telling what a market-determined result will be (even if we know the individual orderings) except to wait and see what the market produces. The market exists as a means by which the social group is able to move from one social state to another as a result of a change in environment without the necessity of making a collective choice. The consistency of the market arises from what Professor Polanyi has called the system of "spontaneous order" embodied in the free enterprise economy. The order "originates in the independent actions of individuals."[28] And, since the order or consistency does originate in the choice process itself, it is meaningless to attempt to construct the ordering. We should not expect to be told in advance what the market will choose. It will choose what it will choose.

The market does not establish the "optimum" social state in the sense that individuals, if called upon to vote politically (act collectively) for or against the market-determined state in opposition to a series of alternatives, would consistently choose it. This may or may not be an important conclusion, depending on the value-judgment made concerning the appropriateness of majority approval as the criterion of "optimum" collective choice. But the essential point here is that the market does not call upon individuals to make a decision collectively at all. This being the case, market choice is just as consistent as, and no more consistent than, the individual choice of which it is composed.

V. SUMMARY

It is necessary to distinguish between the problem of deriving a social welfare function from the individual orderings required for the operation of the decision-making processes of our society and the problem of testing these processes themselves for consistency. I have shown that the failure to make this distinction clear is the source of much of the confusion surrounding the Arrow analysis. A second distinction must be made between social or

28. Michael Polanyi, *The Logic of Liberty* (Chicago: University of Chicago Press, 1951), p. 160.

collective rationality in terms of producing results indicated by a social ordering and the consistency of choice produced by the mechanism of decision-making. If rationality is taken to mean only that the choice-making is consistent, the Arrow analysis shows that voting may be inconsistent. But I have argued that possible inconsistency is a necessary characteristic of orderly majority rule. The market, on the other hand, has been shown to produce consistent choice, in spite of the fact that a "satisfactory social welfare function" cannot be derived from the individual rankings implicit in the market mechanism.

The consistency of market choice is achieved without the overruling of minority values, as would be the case if ordinary political voting were made consistent. Therefore, in a very real sense, market decisions are comparable to political decisions only when unanimity is present. The question as to what extent this lends support to the utilization of the market as the decision-making process when it is a genuine alternative to voting opens up still broader areas of inquiry which cannot be developed here.

IV

INDIVIDUAL CHOICE IN VOTING AND THE MARKET*

THIS paper will compare individual choice in the political voting process and in the market process, with both considered as ideal types. A substantial portion of the analysis will be intuitively familiar to all social scientists, since it serves as a basis for a large part of political theory, on the one hand, and economic theory, on the other. Perhaps as a result of disciplinary specialization, however, the similarities and the differences between these two methods of individual decision-making in liberal society are often overlooked. The state of things is illustrated in the prosaic "one-dollar-one-vote" analogy, which is, at best, only partially appropriate and which tends to conceal extremely important differences.

It is necessary to emphasize the limitations of this analysis. No attempt will be made to compare market choice and voting choice in terms of the relative efficiency in achieving specified social goals or, in other words, as means of *social* decision-making. Many comparisons of this sort have been made. In the great debate over the possibility of rational socialist calculation, the discussion has been concerned primarily with the workability of political decision-making processes when confronted with some social criterion of economic efficiency. The issue has been framed,

* Reprinted without substantial change from the *Journal of Political Economy*, LXII (1954), 334-43. Copyright 1954 by the University of Chicago Press. I am indebted to Marshall Colberg, Jerome Milliman, and Vincent Thursby for helpful comments and suggestions.

appropriately, in terms of the relative efficiency of centralized and decentralized decision-making. Collective choice implies centralized choice, whatever the process of choosing; hence the market has been compared with the whole subset of political choice processes ranging from pure democracy to authoritarian dictatorship.

This paper will compare the *individual* choices involved in the price system and in a single form of centralized decision-making—pure democracy. The individual act of participation in the choice process will be the point of reference. The comparison does not, of course, imply that these two processes will be presented as genuine alternatives to the individual, even in their somewhat less pure forms. A more complete understanding of individual behavior in each process should, however, provide some basis for deciding between the two, if and when they do exist as alternatives.

The following distinctions between individual choice in voting and the market will be discussed: (1) the degree of certainty, (2) the degree of social participation, (3) the degree of responsibility, (4) the nature of the alternatives presented, (5) the degree of coercion, and, finally, (6) the power relations among individuals. Quite obviously, these distinctions are somewhat arbitrarily isolated from one another, and, in a broad sense, each implies others. After these are discussed, some attention will be given to their influence on the selection of voting or the market as a decision-making process for the social group.

I

It will be assumed that the individual chooser possesses the same degree of knowledge concerning the results of alternative decisions in the polling place that he does in the market place.[1]

1. This is a simplifying assumption; there is reason for believing that the individual possesses a greater knowledge of alternatives in the market. This is due, first, to the greater continuity of market choice and, second, to the difference in the degree of knowledge required to compare alternatives in each case. The latter difference has been stressed by Professor Hayek (see F. A. Hayek, "Individualism: True and False," *Individualism and Economic Order* [Chicago: University of Chicago Press, 1948]; see also Robert A. Dahl and Charles E. Lindblom, *Politics, Economics, and Welfare* [New York: Harper & Bros., 1953], p. 63).

It is essential that this assumption be made at this stage, in order that the first important distinction, that of the degree of certainty between individual choice in voting and individual choice in the market, may be made clear.

In market choice the individual is the acting or choosing entity, as well as the entity for which choices are made. In voting, the individual is an acting or choosing entity, but the collectivity is the entity for which decisions are made. The individual in the market can predict with absolute certainty the direct or immediate result of his action. The act of choosing and the consequences of choosing stand in a one-to-one correspondence.[2] On the other hand, the voter, even if he is fully omniscient in his foresight of the consequences of each possible collective decision, can never predict with certainty which of the alternatives presented will be chosen. He can never predict the behavior of other voters in the polling place. Reciprocal behavior prediction of this sort becomes a logical impossibility if individual choice is accepted as meaningful.[3] This inherent uncertainty confronting the voter can perhaps be classified as genuine uncertainty in the Knightian sense; it is not subject to the application of the probability calculus.

This uncertainty must influence to some degree the behavior of the individual in choosing among the possible social alternatives offered to him. Whereas the chooser in the market,[4] assumed to know what he wants, will always take the attainable combination of goods and services standing highest on his preference scale, the voter will not necessarily, or perhaps even probably, choose the alternative most desirable to him. The actual behavior of the voter must be examined within the framework of a theory of choice under uncertainty. As is well known, there is no fully acceptable theory of behavior here, and there are some students of the problem

2. Cf. Kenneth J. Arrow, "Alternative Approaches to the Theory of Choice in Risk-taking Situations," *Econometrica,* XIX (1951), 405.

3. Cf. Frank H. Knight, "Economic Theory and Nationalism," in his *The Ethics of Competition* (London: Allen & Unwin, 1935), p. 340.

4. The device of considering productive services as negatively desired and hence carrying negative prices enables both the buying and the selling activity of the individual to be encompassed in "market choice."

who deny the possibility of rational behavior in uncertain conditions.[5]

II

The second fundamental difference in the two choice processes is found in the sense or degree of participation in *social* decision-making. In the market the individual is confronted with a range of commodities and services, each of which is offered at a given price. Individually, the buyer or seller considers both the range of alternatives and the set of prices to be beyond his power to alter.[6] He is able, therefore, to assume himself apart from, or external to, the social organization which does influence the alternatives made available. He is unconscious of the secondary repercussions of his act of choice which serve to alter the allocation of economic resources.[7] The individual tends to act *as if* all the social variables are determined outside his own behavior, which, in this subjective sense, is *non-participating* and, therefore, *non-social*.[8] The influence of the individual's actual behavior on the ultimate social decision made has no impact upon such behavior.[9]

The individual in the polling place, by contrast, recognizes that his vote is influential in determining the final collective

5. See Arrow, *op. cit.*, for an excellent summary of the various theories of choice under uncertainty.

6. Cf. Ludwig von Mises, *Human Action: A Treatise on Economics* (New Haven: Yale University Press, 1949), p. 312.

7. The fact that individual behavior in the market sets off reactions which are not recognized or intended by the actor, but which do control society's utilization of resources, is stressed in a somewhat different context by Dahl and Lindblom (*op. cit.*, pp. 99-102). They are concerned with the "spontaneous field control" exerted over the individual in this manner. "Control" in this sense, however, is no different from that imposed by the natural environment or any other set of forces external to the individual (see *infra*, Sec. V).

8. For a definition of social action see Max Weber, *The Theory of Social and Economic Organization*, trans. A. M. Henderson and Talcott Parsons (New York: Oxford University Press, 1947), p. 88.

9. It has been advanced as a merit of the price system that it does place the individual in a position of adapting his behavior to the anonymous forces of the market without at the same time feeling that he can participate in changing these forces. On this point see Hayek, *op. cit.*, p. 24.

Market behavior can, of course, become "social" if the individual is made to realize the secondary repercussions of his action. Exceptional cases of such realization may be present even in the perfectly competitive economy, e. g., "buyers' strikes."

choice; he is fully conscious of his participation in social decision-making. The individual act of choosing is, therefore, social, even in a purely subjective sense.

The sense of participation in social choice may exert important effects on the behavior of the individual. It seems probable that the representative individual will act in accordance with a different preference scale when he realizes that he is choosing for the group rather than merely for himself. There are two reasons for this. First, his identification will tend to be broadened,[10] and his "values" will be more likely to influence his ordering of alternatives, whereas in market choice his "tastes" may determine his decision.[11] As an example, the individual may cast a ballot-box vote for the enforcement of prohibition at the same time that he visits his bootlegger, without feeling that he is acting inconsistently. Even if the individual's welfare horizon is not modified in a shift from market to voting choice, or vice versa, there is a second, and perhaps equally important, reason for a rearrangement of his preference scale and hence for some difference in behavior. The individual's ranking of alternatives in market choice assumes no action on the part of other individuals in specific correspondence to his own. In voting, the choice is determined from a ranking of alternative situations in each of which the position of the individual is collectively determined for him and for *all* other individuals in the group.[12] As an example of this difference, businessmen in a perfectly competitive industry marketing a product with an inelastic demand may vote to approve governmentally-imposed production limitations, while, if left to operate independently, they would have no incentive to restrict production. A further example may be used to illustrate the case in which both these effects on individual choice may be operative. A man who in the unregulated market economy would construct a billboard advertising his product might vote for the abolition of billboards because he considers such action preferable in terms of group welfare and/or because

10. Dahl and Lindblom, *op. cit.*, p. 422.

11. Cf. Kenneth J. Arrow, *Social Choice and Individual Values* (New York: John Wiley & Sons, 1951), p. 82.

12. Cf. William J. Baumol, *Welfare Economics and Theory of the State* (Cambridge: Harvard University Press, 1952), p. 15; Trygve Haavelmo, "The Notion of Involuntary Economic Decisions," *Econometrica*, XVIII (1950), 3, 8.

his own interest will be better served by such collectively imposed action.

III

The difference in the individual's sense of social participation has its obverse, however, which may be introduced as a third distinction between the voting and market processes. Since voting implies collective choice, the responsibility for making any particular social or collective decision is necessarily divided. This seems clearly to affect the individual's interest in the choosing process. Since a decision is to be made in any case, the single individual need not act at all; he may abstain from voting while other individuals act.

The responsibility for market decisions is uniquely concentrated on the chooser; there can be no abstention. There is a tangible benefit as well as a cost involved in each market chooser's decision, while there is neither an immediately realizable and certain benefit nor an imputable cost normally involved in the voter's choice.[13] This difference tends to guarantee that a more precise and objective consideration of alternative costs takes place in the minds of individuals choosing in the market. This does not suggest, however, that the greater precision in the consideration of alternatives by individuals in the market implies that the costs and benefits taken into account are necessarily the proper ones from a "social" point of view.[14]

It seems quite possible that in many instances the apparent placing of "the public interest" above mere individual or group interest in political decisions represents nothing more than a failure of the voters to consider fully the real costs of the activity to be undertaken. It is extremely difficult to determine whether the affirmative vote of a non-beneficiary individual for a public welfare project implies that he is either acting socially in accordance with a "nobler" ordering of alternatives or is estimating his own self-

13. On this point see Alfred C. Neal, "The 'Planning Approach' in Public Economy," *Quarterly Journal of Economics,* LIV (1940), 251.

14. In cases where spill-over effects are significant, the costs taken into account by the individual in the market will clearly exclude some important elements of social costs (positive or negative) which should be considered in the making of a social decision (see Dahl and Lindblom, *op. cit.,* p. 419).

interest in accordance with a "collective-action" preference scale, or whether it suggests that he has failed to weigh adequately the opportunity costs of the project.

The difference in responsibility provides a basis for Professor Mises' argument that an individual is "less corruptible" in the market.[15] This might plausibly be advanced without necessarily contradicting the claim that ballot-box choice, if uncorrupted, is made in accordance with a more inclusive and modified value scale. A somewhat related point has been made by Professor Spengler when he says that there is, in voting as compared with the market, "the tendency of the individual (especially when he is a part of a large and disciplined organization) more easily to lose . . . political than economic autonomy."[16]

IV

A fourth distinction, and perhaps one of the most important, between individual choice in voting and the market lies in the nature of the alternatives offered to the individual in each case. Choice implies that alternatives are mutually conflicting; otherwise, all would be chosen, which is equivalent to saying that none would be chosen. It is in the precise way in which the alternatives mutually conflict that the voting process must be sharply distinguished from the market mechanism.

Alternatives of market choice normally conflict only in the sense that the law of diminishing returns is operative. This is true at the level both of the individual chooser and of the social group. If an individual desires *more* of a particular commodity or service, the market normally requires only that he take *less* of another commodity or service. If all individuals, through their market choices, indicate that *more* resources should be devoted to the production of a particular commodity, this requires only that *less* resources be devoted to the production of other commodities.

15. Ludwig von Mises, *Socialism,* new ed. (New Haven: Yale University Press, 1951), p. 21.

16. J. J. Spengler, "Generalists versus Specialists in Social Science: An Economist's View," *American Political Science Review,* XLIV (1950), 378.

Alternatives of voting choice are more normally mutually exclusive, that is, the selection of one precludes the selection of another. This, too, is true at the level both of the individual chooser and of the whole system. The individual voter normally faces mutually exclusive choices because of the indivisibility of his vote. Group choices tend to be mutually exclusive by the very nature of the alternatives, which are regularly of the "all-or-none" variety.

For the individual, market choice amounts to the allocation of an unspecialized and highly divisible resource (income-yielding capacity) among a range of alternatives. On the other hand, few voting schemes include means which enable an individual to break his total voting strength down into fractional parts. The attribute of scarcity has never been applied to voting strength; an additional vote is granted to each individual when each new collective decision is made. To make market choice similar to voting in this respect, each individual would be required to devote his whole capacity in each market period to one commodity or service. If only the buying side is taken into account, this means that the consumer's whole expenditure should be on one commodity. It seems clear that this feature of the choice process can itself affect the nature of the alternatives presented. If the individual were required to spend the whole of his income on one commodity, market alternatives would tend to become mutually exclusive and to become severely limited in number and variety. Most of the normally available goods and services would disappear from the market places.

The major share of the difference in the nature of the alternatives presented in the two choice processes must, however, be attributed to fundamental differences in the objects of choice themselves. In a very real sense many voting choices can never be made in the market because they are inherently more difficult, involving, as they do, considerations which cannot be taken into account effectively by the individual choosing only for himself. The choice to be made is normally among two or more alternatives, only one of which may be chosen, with its very selection precluding the selection of the others. Even if the results of the voting were to be based upon the proportionate number of votes cast for each alternative, combination or composite solutions of the market type would not be possible in most cases. Inherent in the market solution, by contrast, is choice among an almost infinite number of *combinations* of goods and services, in each of which some of almost every conceivable good and service will be included.[17] As a result of this difference, individual choice in the market can be more articulate than in the voting booth.

V

There follows directly from the difference in the nature of alternatives an extremely important fifth distinction between the voting process and the market process as faced by the individual choice-maker. If production indivisibilities may be disregarded (they would not be present in the ideally competitive world), each dollar vote in the market becomes positively effective[18] to the individual, not only in providing him with a unit of the chosen commodity or service, but also in generating changes in the economic environment. In either of these senses a dollar vote is never overruled; the individual is never placed in the position of being a member of a dissenting minority.[19] When a commodity or service is exchanged in the market, the individual chooses from among *existing* alternatives; at the secondary stage, of which he is unconscious, his behavior tends to direct economic resources in a specific manner.

In voting, the individual does not choose among *existing* but rather among *potential* alternatives, and, as mentioned earlier, he is never secure in his belief that his vote will count positively. He may lose his vote and be placed in the position of having cast his vote in opposition to the alternative finally chosen by the social group. He may be compelled to accept a result contrary

17. The market is thus the only system of proportional representation which will likely work at all (cf. Clarence Philbrook, "Capitalism and the Rule of Love," *Southern Economic Journal,* XIX [1953], 466).

18. A decision to sell productive services may be considered as a vote for generalized purchasing power (i.e., dollars), and thus may be considered positively effective if the sale is consummated.

19. For an excellent summary discussion of this point see Von Mises, *Human Action: A Treatise on Economics,* p. 271.

to his expressed preference. A similar sort of coercion is never present in market choice. It has been argued that pressure toward social conformity "compels those outvoted to make an expenditure against their will."[20] While it is no doubt true that both the individual's earning and expenditure patterns are conditioned to a large degree by the average patterns of his social group, the distinction between this indirectly coercive effect involved in the social urge to conform and the direct and unavoidable coercion involved in collective decision seems an extremely important one.

If the assumption of production divisibility is relaxed, some modifications of this conclusion must be made. Given the presence of indivisibility, the individual's dollar vote may be overruled at the secondary stage of the market choice process. On the buying side, if the consumer's dollar vote is not accompanied by enough other votes to maintain the production of the particular good or service, it may be "lost," and, at this stage, the buyer may be in a position apparently equivalent to that of the ballot-box supporter of the losing side of an issue. On the selling side, if there are not enough final demand dollar votes to warrant production of those commodities or services embodying the individual's productive contribution, then the attempt to convert productive services into generalized purchasing power on former terms may be thwarted. But in each case, at the initial or primary stage of the market process, the individual's expressed choice is never overruled. The buyer would never have possessed the opportunity to choose, had not the commodity or service been existent in the market; and the seller of productive services would have never been able to develop particular skills, had not a derived demand for those skills been present. And since the one-to-one correspondence between the act of choice and its result is the only condition directly influencing the individual's behavior, there can never be present the sense of directly losing one's market vote. There may, of course, arise a sense of regret when the consumer returns to the market place and finds a desired commodity no longer available

20. Dahl and Lindblom, *op. cit.*, p. 424. A similar position is taken by Professor Howard Bowen (see his *Toward Social Economy* [New York: Rinehart & Co., 1948], p. 44).

and when the individual no longer is able to market productive services previously adapted to particular uses. The consumer may also regret that certain desired goods have never been placed in the market in the first place, and the individual seller may be concerned that there has never existed a ready market for his peculiar talents. This sort of regret does not, however, apply uniquely to market choice. It applies equally to political voting, and it does not, therefore, constitute the market's equivalent of the "lost" ballot-box vote. It is true that there may be commodities and services not offered for sale which the individual would be willing to purchase, but there may also be many potential alternatives never presented for a vote which an individual might desire to support.

VI

Each of the five preceding distinctions in the individual participation in voting and market choice is present even when the relative power positions of individuals are made equivalent in the two processes, that is, when there is absolute equality in the distribution of income-earning capacity among market choosers. All these distinctions tend, therefore, to be neglected in the simple "one-dollar-one-vote" analogy, which concentrates attention only upon the difference in the relative power of individuals. Market choice is normally conducted under conditions of inequality among individuals, while voting tends, at least ideally, to be conducted under conditions of equality.

The essential point to be emphasized in this connection is that the inequalities present in market choice are inequalities in individual power and not in individual freedom, if care is taken to define freedom and power in such a way as to maximize the usefulness of these two concepts in discussion. As Professor Knight has suggested, it seems desirable for this reason to define freedom somewhat narrowly as the absence of coercion and unfreedom as the state of being prevented from utilizing the normally available capacities for action.[21]

21. See Frank H. Knight, "The Meaning of Freedom," in *The Philosophy of American Democracy,* ed. Charles M. Perry (Chicago: University of Chicago Press, 1943), p. 64; "Conflict of Values: Freedom and Justice," in *Goals of*

VII

There remains the task of evaluating the foregoing differences in the position of the individual chooser in voting and in the market, with a view toward determining the relative appropriateness of the two choice processes for the social group when they are, in fact, possible alternatives. If rationality in individual behavior is considered a desirable feature of a choice process,[22] there would appear to be several reasons for claiming that market choice should be preferred. The greater degree of certainty seems clearly to produce more rational behavior; the uniquely centered responsibility tends to work in the same direction. Even if voting and the market are genuinely alternative means of making choices in a particular situation (thereby eliminating the inherent difficulties in voting choice when this is the only alternative), the difference in the divisibility of voting tends to make market choices finer and more articulate. The fact that market choice tends to embody greater rationality in *individual behavior* than does voting choice does not suggest that market choice tends to produce greater *social* rationality.[23]

The market should also be preferred as a choice process when individual freedom is considered in isolation. The absence of negative results of individual choices and, therefore, the absence of the direct coercion which requires the individual to accept unchosen alternatives, makes for a greater degree of freedom in market choice.

On the other hand, voting should perhaps be preferred to the market when individual motivation in choice is the attribute examined. Voting choice does provide individuals with a greater

Economic Life, ed. Dudley Ward (New York: Harper & Bros., 1953), pp. 207, 226. For supporting views see Michael Polanyi, *The Logic of Liberty* (Chicago: University of Chicago Press, 1951), p. 159; E. F. Carritt, *Morals and Politics* (London: Oxford University Press, 1953), pp. 195 ff.

22. Rationality in individual behavior is defined in the normal manner, that is, the individual is able to rank alternatives, and such ranking is transitive.

23. It is on this basis that Dahl and Lindblom appear to reject the argument that market choice is more rational (*op. cit.,* chap. xv). They do so because they are concerned with rationality in the social sense, defined as that action which maximizes the achievement of certain postulated social goals. If rationality is defined purely in terms of individual behavior, their argument appears to support that of this paper, although they seem explicitly to deny this at one point (*ibid.,* p. 422).

sense of participation in social decision-making, and, in this way, it may bring forth the "best" in man and tend to make individuals take somewhat more account of the "public interest." This attribute of the voting process has probably been somewhat neglected by liberal students and somewhat overemphasized in importance by socialists. It should be noted, however, that, even if this proves to be an important difference, voting will produce consistent or "rational" *social* choice only if men are able to agree on the ultimate social goals.[24] If men are not able to agree on what is genuine morality, the adoption of a choice process in which they act more morally cannot be justified on this ground.[25]

It is in the power structure among individuals antecedent to choice that the market may, and most often does, prove unacceptable. Political voting is characterized by an alternative power structure which may be deemed preferable to that of the market. And the selection of the one-for-one power relation among individuals appears to carry with it the selection of voting over market choice. If, however, the market power structure can be effectively modified independently of the choice process, this apparent advantage of political voting need not be present.

It should be noted that the fundamental decision to modify the power structure, as well as the extent of such modification, clearly must be made by the ballot box. And in this type of decision especially it is essential that individuals act in accordance with a value-ordering which is somewhat different from that motivating individual market choice. After a redistributive decision for the group is made, it must be further decided whether a particular choice shall be made by the market or by political voting. This decision on process must also be made by means of the ballot box. In this decision the market should be rejected only if individual market choices are considered by voters to produce a social state less desirable than that which is produced by individual voting choices.

24. Cf. Arrow, *Social Choice and Individual Values.*

25. If they cannot agree, the possible irrationality of collective choice may be a desirable rather than an undesirable feature, since rationality could be imposed only at the cost of minority coercion (see "Social Choice, Democracy, and Free Markets," Essay III, *supra*).

The selection of the choice process, if the redistributive decision can be made separately, will depend to a large degree upon the relative positions of the various social goals in the value scales of individuals comprising the voting group. If consistency in individual behavior and individual freedom are highly regarded relative to other values, the market will tend to be favored. If, on the other hand, the somewhat vague, even though meaningful, concept of "social welfare" is the overriding consideration, voting choice may be preferred. But even here, if the individual's expressed interest is judged to be the best index of social welfare, the market may still be acceptable as a choice process (this was essentially the position of the utilitarians).

The selection of the choice process will also depend on whether or not the voters consider their own self-interest to be better served individualistically or collectively. If the "collective-action" preference scale allows the required majority of individuals to attain a more esteemed position than does the "individual-action" preference scale, voting choice will be selected regardless of the ranking of social goals. In this case it might be irrational for an individual to choose the market process, even though his behavior in the market, once this process was selected by the group, would be more rational than his behavior in the voting booth. The electorate should select the ballot box over the market place in those areas where individually determined market acts tend to produce results which are in conflct either with those which a large group of voters estimate to be their own or the "social" welfare and where the conflict is significant enough to warrant the sacrifice both of the individual freedom and the individual rationality involved.

In so far as market choice must be made under imperfectly competitive conditions[26] and voting choice under conditions of less than "pure" democracy, the analysis of individual behavior in each process must be appropriately modified and the conclusions reached earlier changed accordingly. No attempt will be made here to extend the analysis in this direction.

26. Imperfections include, of course, the presence of such monetary and structural factors as may lead to unemployment.

VIII

A major source of confusion in the discussion of economic policy stems from the failure to distinguish carefully between the selection of the power structure among individual choosers and the selection of the choice mechanism. This arises from the more fundamental failure to define freedom in such a way that market freedom and market power may be differentiated conceptually.[27] In many real world situations the market power structure cannot be effectively modified independently; that is, a redistributive decision cannot be made in isolation. It is nevertheless essential for analytical clarity that this ideational distinction be made.

The separation of the power structure and the decision-making process is less inclusive and less complex than the similar and more commonly encountered distinction between the "income" and the "resource" aspects of economic policy. The problem of selecting the desirable structure of power relations among individuals in the market is, of course, equivalent to the income problem, broadly considered. The "resource" side of the "income-resource" dichotomy introduces an evaluation of policy in terms of the social criteria of economic efficiency, and these aspects of the market mechanism tend to be emphasized. The "choice" side of the "power-choice" dichotomy which has been developed here tends to concentrate attention upon individual behavior in making choices, and it tends to emphasize the greater range of freedom allowed the individual, as well as the greater degree of individual rationality, in market choice.

27. This constitutes one of the major weaknesses in Dahl and Lindblom's otherwise excellent comparison of voting and the market (*op. cit.*, pp. 414-27).

V

POSITIVE ECONOMICS, WELFARE ECONOMICS, AND POLITICAL ECONOMY*

ECONOMIC theory, as we know it, was developed largely by utilitarians. Admitting the measurability and interpersonal comparability of utility and accepting the maximization of utility as an ethically desirable social goal, neo-classical economists were able to combine an instinctively human zeal for social reform with subjectively satisfactory scientific integrity. The positivist revolution has sharply disturbed this scholarly equilibrium. If utility is neither cardinally measurable nor comparable among persons, the economist who seeks to remain "pure" must proceed with caution in discussing social policy. The "positive" economist becomes an inventor of testable hypotheses, and his professional place in policy formation becomes wholly indirect.

Milton Friedman has provided the clearest statement of the positivist position,[1] and he has called for a distinct separation between the scientific and the non-scientific behavior of individuals calling themselves economists. But economics, as a discipline, will probably continue to attract precisely those scholars who desire to assist in policy formation and to do so professionally. The social role of the economist remains that of securing more intelligent legislation; and the incremental additions to the state of knowledge which "positive" economics may make seem to shut off too

* Reprinted without substantial change from the *Journal of Law and Economics,* II (1959), 124-38.

1. Milton Friedman, *Essays in Positive Economics* (Chicago: University of Chicago Press, 1953), pp. 3-43.

large an area of discussion from his professional competence. Does there exist a role for the political economist as such? This essay will examine this question and suggest an approach.[2]

I. THE NEW WELFARE ECONOMICS

The "new" welfare economics was born in response to the challenge posed by the positivist revolution. The intellectual source of this sub-discipline is Pareto, whose earlier attempts to introduce scientific objectivity into the social studies led him to enunciate the now-famous definition of "optimality" or "efficiency." This definition states that any situation is "optimal" if all possible moves from it result in some individual's being made worse off. The definition may be transformed into a rule which states that any social change is desirable which results in (1) everyone being better off, or, (2) someone being better off and no one being worse off than before the change. This Pareto rule is itself an ethical proposition, a value statement, but it is one which requires a minimum of premises and one which should command wide assent. The rule specifically eliminates the requirement that interpersonal comparisons of utility be made. As stated, however, a fundamental ambiguity remains in the rule. Some objective content must be given to the terms "better off" and "worse off." This is accomplished by equating "better off" with "in that position voluntarily chosen." Individual preferences are taken to indicate changes in individual well-being, and a man is said to be better off when he voluntarily changes his position from A to B when he could have remained in A.

The theoretical work completed during the past twenty years has consisted, first of all, in a refinement and development of the Paretian conditions for "optimality." Much attention has been given to a careful and precise definition of the necessary and sufficient attributes of a social situation to insure its qualification as a Paretian P-point, that is, a point on the "optimality surface." The application of this theoretical apparatus has taken two lines

2. The approach which will be suggested here involves an extension of some of Wicksell's ideas on fiscal theory to modern welfare economics. For a recently published translation of Wicksell's fiscal theory, see "A New Principle of Just Taxation," in *Classics in the Theory of Public Finance,* ed. by R. A. Musgrave and A. T. Peacock (London: Macmillan, 1958), pp. 72-118.

of development. The first, which is sometimes more specifically called the "new welfare economics," is an attempt to devise tests which will allow changes in social situations to be evaluated. This work, which has been associated with Kaldor, Hicks, and Scitovsky, includes the discussion of the "compensation principle" and the distinction between actual and potential increases in "welfare." The second line of development has been, in one sense, a critique of the Kaldor-Hicks approach. The ethical purity of the compensation tests proposed has been questioned, and additional ethical norms have been deliberately re-introduced through the device of a "social welfare function" which, conceptually, orders all possible states of society. With this, the problem of genuine choice among alternatives disappears, and the single "best" state of the world may be selected. This function may take any form, but its users have normally conceived the Paretian conditions to be relevant in defining a preliminary subset of social configurations. This approach, which is associated with Bergson, Samuelson, and Graaff, now appears to have more widespread support than the alternative one. Its supporters, notably Samuelson, argue that the Kaldor-Hicks efforts were "misguided" and erroneous,[3] and that only the "social welfare function" construction offers real promise of further development. In the latter, allegedly, "the foundation is laid for the 'economics of the good society.' "[4]

II. OMNISCIENCE AND EFFICIENCY

Welfare economists, new and old, have generally assumed omniscience in the observer, although the assumption is rarely made explicit and even more rarely are its implications examined.[5] The observing economist is considered able to "read" individual preference functions. Thus, even though an "increase in welfare" for an individual is defined as "that which he chooses," the economist can unambiguously distinguish an increase in welfare inde-

3. Paul A. Samuelson, "Comment," *A Survey of Contemporary Economics,* Vol. II, ed. by B. F. Haley (American Economic Association, 1952), p. 37.

4. Paul A. Samuelson, "Social Indifference Curves," *Quarterly Journal of Economics,* LXX (1956), 22.

5. J. de V. Graaff makes the assumption explicitly, but after one short paragraph proceeds with his argument. See *Theoretical Welfare Economics* (Cambridge: Cambridge University Press, 1957), p. 13.

pendent of individual behavior because he can accurately predict what the individual would, in fact, "choose" if confronted with the alternatives under consideration.

This omniscience assumption seems wholly unacceptable. Utility is measurable, ordinally or cardinally, only to the individual decision-maker. It is a *subjectively* quantifiable magnitude. While the economist may be able to make certain presumptions about "utility" on the basis of observed facts about behavior, he must remain fundamentally ignorant concerning the actual ranking of alternatives until and unless that ranking is revealed by the overt action of the individual in choosing.

If a presumption of ignorance replaces that of omniscience, the way in which "efficiency" as a norm enters into the economist's schemata must be drastically modified. No "social" value scale can be constructed from individual preference patterns since the latter are revealed only through behavior. Hence "efficiency" cannot be defined independently; it cannot be instrumentally employed as a criterion for social action. Discussions of "ideal output" and "maximization of real income" become meaningless when it is recognized that the economizing process includes as data *given ends* as conceived by individuals. Ends are not *given* for the social group in any sense appropriate to the solution of problems in political economy, and the normally accepted definition of the economizing problem is seriously incomplete in not having made this clear.

"Efficiency" in the sense of maximizing a payoff or outcome from the use of limited resources is meaningless without some common denominator, some value scale, against which various possible results can be measured. To the individual decision-maker the concept of an "efficiency criterion" is a useful one, but to the independent observer the pitfalls of omniscience must be carefully avoided. The observer may introduce an efficiency criterion only through *his own estimate of his subjects' value scales.* Hence the maximization criterion which the economist may employ is wholly in terms of his own estimate of the value scales of individuals other than himself. *Presumptive efficiency* is, therefore, the appropriate conception for usage in political economy.

The relationship of the *presumptive efficiency* criterion to the Paretian construction remains to be clarified. Given the assumption of ignorance, Paretian "efficiency" cannot be employed in aiding a group in choosing from among a set of possible social policy changes. A specific change may be judged to be Pareto-optimal or "efficient" only after it has, in fact, been proposed and the individual preferences for or against the change revealed. Nevertheless, in discussing proposals before individual preferences are revealed, the economist may utilize a *presumed efficiency* notion which retains the Paretian features. In diagnosing a specific proposal, the economist makes a judgment as to its "efficiency" on the basis of *his own* estimate of individual preferences. The Paretian elements are retained in the sense that the observer makes no attempt to do other than to "translate" what he considers to be individual preferences. He accepts these preferences, or tastes, as *he thinks they exist*. He does not evaluate social alternatives on the basis of individual preferences as he thinks they should be.

This characteristic behavior of the political economist is, or should be, ethically neutral; the indicated results are influenced by his own value scale only in so far as this reflects his membership in the larger group. Conceptually, the economist may present a social policy change as "presumed Pareto-optimal," the results of which are wholly indifferent to him as an individual member of society. The propositions which the economist is able to develop through the procedure outlined are operational in the modern sense of this term. The presentation of a policy shift is a hypothesis concerning the structure of individual values and is subject to conceptual contradiction. The failure of recent methodological discussion to recognize this operational aspect of political economy appears to be based on an attempt to place the practitioner in a false position in the decision-making complex. The political economist is often conceived as being able to *recommend* policy A over policy B. If, as we have argued above, no objective social criterion exists, the economist *qua* scientist is unable to recommend. Therefore, any policy discussion on his part appears to take on normative implications. But there does exist a positive role for the economist in the formation of policy. His task is that of diagnosing social situations and presenting to the choosing individuals a set of possible changes. He does not recommend policy A over policy B. He presents policy A as a hypothesis subject to testing. The hypothesis is that policy A will in fact, prove to be Pareto-optimal. The conceptual test is *consensus* among members of the choosing group, not objective improvement in some measurable social aggregate.

Political economy is thus "positivistic" in a different sense from the more narrowly-conceived positive economics. Both allow the expert to make certain predictions about the real world, predictions which are operationally meaningful. Propositions of positive economics find their empirical support or refutation in observable economic quantities or in observable market behavior of individuals. Political economy differs in that its propositions find empirical support or refutation in the observable behavior of individuals *in their capacities as collective decision makers,* in other words, in politics.

Propositions advanced by political economists must always be considered as tentative hypotheses offered as solutions to social problems. The subjective bases for these propositions should emphasize the necessity for their being considered as alternatives which may or may not be accepted. But this is not to suggest that one proposition is equally good with all others. Just as is the case with positive economics, the skill of the observer and his capacity in drawing upon the experience which has been accumulated will determine the relative success of his predictions.

There are no fully appropriate analogies to this task of the political economist, but the role of the medical diagnostician perhaps comes closest. The patient is observed to be ill; a remedy is prescribed. This remedy is a hypothesis advanced by the diagnostician. If the illness persists, an alternative remedy is suggested and the first hypothesis discarded. The process continues until the patient is restored to health or the existence of no solution is accepted. While this analogy is helpful, it can also be misleading. In political economy, the observer isolates an "illness" or rather what he believes to be an "illness" through his knowledge of the system. He presents a possible change. But this change is a "cure" only if *consensus* is attained in its support. The measure of "wellness" for the political economist is not improvement in an independently observable characteristic but rather agreement. If no agreement can be attained, the presumed "illness" persists and the political economist must search for still other possible solutions. The political behavior of individuals, not market performance or results, provides the criteria for testing hypotheses of political economy.

III. COMPENSATION AND EXTERNALITY

The "welfare economics" suggested here is simpler than that which assumes omniscience on the part of the observer. Much of the discussion in the sub-discipline has been devoted to two problems, both of which will be substantially eliminated in the approach suggested. First, the appropriateness or inappropriateness of compensation has been a central topic along with the discussion of the legitimacy or illegitimacy of certain tests. But quite clearly if the political economist is presumed to be ignorant of individual preference fields, his predictions (as embodied in suggested social policy changes) can only be supported or refuted if full compensation is, in fact, paid. The potential compensation argument disappears, and the whole controversy over the appropriate tests becomes meaningless at this level of argument.

Many scholars have objected to the requirement that compensation be paid on the grounds that such requirement creates a serious bias toward the initial or status quo distribution of "welfare" among individuals of the group. This criticism seems misdirected and inapplicable if the purposes of compensation are conceived to be those outlined. Full compensation is essential, not in order to maintain any initial distribution on ethical grounds, but in order to decide which one from among the many possible social policy changes does, in fact, satisfy the genuine Pareto rule. Compensation is the only device available to the political economist for this purpose.

To be sure, if the observing economist is assumed omniscient, the actual payment of compensation may seem unnecessary, and the requirement for payment may appear to introduce the bias mentioned. No additional information about individual preference fields is needed, and none can be revealed by behavior. The proposed change is no longer a hypothesis to be tested, and the relatively neutral ethics imposed by the Pareto rule may prove too restrictive. And if the observer does not move in the direction of the Bergson-Samuelson welfare function, he may attempt to devise tests for potential compensation. In this way the whole debate about the Kaldor-Hicks-Scitovsky criteria for improvement has arisen. This approach constitutes a distortion of the Pareto rule. If ethical evaluations on the part of the observer are to be introduced, there is no place for the Pareto rule. This rule is designed for use in situations where individual values must count, not because they possess some inherent ethical superiority (which is quite a different point) but because individual action provides the only guide toward acceptable collective action.

The full compensation requirement need not imply, indeed it will not normally imply, the maintenance of the status quo in the distribution of either income or welfare. Presumably, if a given social change is approved by all parties, each must be better off in absolute terms. Therefore, at the simplest level of discussion, there is more "welfare" to go around than before the change. To be sure, the relative distribution of "welfare" may be modified significantly by a fully compensated change. This is true because the order of presentation will determine the final point chosen from among a whole subset of acceptable points. The political economist cannot, however, say anything concerning the relative merits of the separate points in this subset. This amounts to saying that the political economist's task is completed when he has shown the parties concerned that there exist mutual gains "from trade." He has no function in suggesting specific contract terms within the bargaining range itself.

An additional simple, but often overlooked, point on compensation needs to be made. The requirement of full compensation as here interpreted need not imply that the measured incomes of individuals or groups may not be reduced by acceptable social policy changes. "Welfare" is defined as that which is expressed by individual preference as revealed in behavior. And individual behavior may be fully consistent with a reduction in measured personal income or wealth. For example, a policy which combines progressive income taxation and public expenditure on the social services may command unanimous support even though the process involves a reduction in the measured real incomes of the rich. The existence of voluntary charity indicates that individuals are, in fact, willing to reduce their own incomes in order to increase those of others. And the peculiar nature of collective choice makes support for collective or governmental action perhaps even more likely. Many individuals may find themselves saying: "I should be willing to support this proposal provided that other equally-situated individuals do likewise." Thus, collective action may command relatively widespread support whereas no purely voluntary action might be taken in its absence.[6]

A second major problem which has concerned theorists in welfare economics recently has been the possible existence of external effects in individual consumption and production decisions, sometimes called spillover or neighborhood effects. But this annoying complication also disappears in the approach to welfare economics suggested here. If, in fact, external effects are present, these will be fully reflected in the individual choices made for or against the collective action which may be proposed. External effects which are unaccounted for in the presumptive efficiency criterion of the economist and the proposal based upon this criterion will negate the prediction of consensus represented in the alternative suggested. The presence of such effects on a large scale will, of course, make the task of the political economist more difficult. His predictions must embody estimates of a wider range of individual preferences than would otherwise be the case. The compensations included in the suggested policy changes must be more carefully drawn and must be extended to include more individuals who might otherwise be neglected.[7]

6. This point has been stressed by Baumol. See W. J. Baumol, *Welfare Economics and the Theory of the State* (Cambridge, Massachusetts: Harvard University Press, 1952).

7. The discussion of this paragraph assumes that the membership in the group making the collective choice is at least as large as the "neighborhood" defined by the presence of external effects.

Both the compensation and externality problems may be illustrated by reference to the classical example of the smoking chimney. The economist observes what he considers to be smoke damage and discontent among families living adjacent to the smoke-creating plant. Using a presumptive efficiency criterion, he suggests a possible course of action which the group may take. This action must include, on the one hand, the payment of some tax by the previously-damaged individuals who stand to gain by the change. On the other hand, the action must include some subsidization of the owners of the firm to compensate them for the capital loss which is to be imposed by the rule or law which states that henceforward the full "social" costs of the operation must be shouldered. Some such tax-compensation–smoke-abatement scheme will command unanimous consent from the group which includes both individuals living within the damaged area and the owners of the firm. The problem for the political economist is that of searching out and locating from among the whole set of possible combinations one which will prove acceptable to all parties. If the smoke nuisance is a real one, at least one such alternative must exist. If no agreement of this sort is possible, the economist can only conclude that the presumptive efficiency criterion was wrongly conceived and the hypothesis based upon it falsified.[8]

IV. THE SCOPE FOR POLITICAL ECONOMY

The scope for application of the "positive" political economy suggested must now be considered, for unless this is done the

8. Objections will be raised to the procedure suggested here because its acceptance seems to leave the door open to exploitation of some parties to the contract by other unscrupulous parties. The owners of the smoke-creating firm may refuse to agree to any scheme except the one which grants them compensation equal to the full benefits of the proposed change. This possibility, or its converse, exists. But in refusing to agree to any proffered compensation equal to or above the estimated value of the capital losses undergone, the owners must recognize that such opportunities might not recur.

As a second point, if the distributional results of a change are significantly important, this fact alone may reduce the extent of the bargaining range. Even though the objectively-measured "income" of the previously-damaged group were demonstrably increased by the adoption of the tax-compensation–smoke-abatement plan, this group might not agree if the owners secured the predominant share of the total benefits. They might veto the plan on distributional grounds, thereby preventing unanimity.

procedure may appear to stultify much desirable social change. The main point which needs to be made is that the political economist is properly concerned only with changes in the law. He is not concerned with the enforcement of existing law (at least in his professional capacity as political economist) or with social changes which take place within an existing legal framework. This limitation severely restricts the applicability of the compensation procedure outlined, and, in so doing, makes the procedure more useful as a guide to action. Changes in "law" must be compensated because only through the compensation device can appropriate criteria for "improvement" be discovered. But within the structure of existing law, no grounds for compensation exist. This point is illustrated by reference to the theft example used by Stigler in his critique of the new welfare economics.[9] Could not the "real income" of society be increased by bribing potential thieves instead of hiring policemen? This question is irrelevant. Presumably, those individuals who are thieves at any moment have supported laws which are designed to prevent theft. Stealing is a recognized violation of existing law, and, as such, deserves punishment without compensation. Quite clearly no consensus could be expected on a proposed change in the law which would involve bribing the thieves. The suggestion that such a change might increase "real income" implies some objective definition of real income which is independent of individuals' behavior.

A more practical example involves government's prosecution of monopoly. The capital losses which are imposed upon firms successfully prosecuted should not, normally, be offset by compensation. This is because such action involves, in principle, no law making. By contrast, the removal of a specific exemption to the law should be accompanied by the appropriate compensating action.

There are, of course, difficult problems involved in distinguishing between changes in law and the enforcement of existing law.

9. George Stigler, "The New Welfare Economics," *American Economic Review*, XXXIII (1943), 355-59.

But such problems are no different from those normally faced in the everyday definition of property rights, which are, of course, enormously difficult. The whole issue here may well be phrased in terms of property rights. The political economist in the specific role discussed here is concerned with social or collective action which modifies in some way the structure of legitimate property rights. Compensation is required for the reasons suggested above. On the other hand, law enforcement may modify the structure of actual property rights, but, in principle, it does not disturb legitimate rights.

Political economy appropriately deals only with one form of social change, namely that which is deliberately chosen by the members of the social group in their collective capacities. Changes may occur for many reasons, and the set of possible changes which constitutes the domain of political economy is a relatively small subset of this total. Therefore, the requirement of compensation necessary to insure consensus or unanimity is not open to the commonly-voiced objection that all progress involves social disturbance, that some individuals must be injured and others benefited by any significant social upheaval.

Changes may occur through shifts in tastes, introduction of new techniques, or growth in the supply of basic resources. These are normally considered to be the means through which an economy "progresses" or "grows." Changes of this nature are, however, different, philosophically, from those which are deliberately imposed through collective action. And the distinction is important. The free-market economic order is organized on the assumption that shifts may occur in the fundamentally exogenous variables: wants, resources, and technology. Imperfections of knowledge about the possible shifts in these variables are incorporated with the appropriate offsetting entrepreneurial rewards and punishments. Any attempt to secure unanimous consent through a compensation scheme for all economic changes would destroy the system. But changes imposed by collective action are different, and the uncertainty involved in attempts to predict such action cannot be discounted or offset in the ordinary market structure.

V. THE SOCIAL WELFARE FUNCTION

The approach to political economy suggested in this essay may be compared with the Bergson-Samuelson approach which deliberately introduces ethical evaluations in the form of the "social welfare function." Both approaches aim at establishing a role for the economist *qua* scientist beyond positive economics narrowly defined. The differences between the two approaches lie in the treatment of individual values.

The "social welfare function" is an explicit expression of a value criterion. It incorporates fully the required information concerning the relative importance of conflicting aims, including the relative importance of separate individuals within the social group. The function orders all possible social situations and allows an external observer to select one as "best." Presumably this "best" point will lie on a "welfare frontier" which contains a sub-infinity of possible points. But the precise meaning of this "welfare frontier" is not entirely clear. If social situations are to be ordered *externally,* the "individual welfare scales" embodied must be those akin to those which enter into the presumptive efficiency criterion discussed above. Individual preferences, in so far as they enter the construction (and they need not do so) must be those which *appear to the observer* rather than those revealed by the behavior of the individuals themselves. In other words, even if the value judgments expressed in the function say that individual preferences are to count, these preferences must be those presumed by the observer rather than those revealed in behavior.

Several questions may be raised. Unless the relevant choices are to be made by some entity other than individuals themselves, why is there any need to construct a "social" value scale? There would seem to be no reason for making interpersonal comparisons of "welfare" based on hypothetical individual preferences except for the purpose of assisting in the attainment of *given ends* for the group or some sub-group. This central feature of the approach seems, therefore, to be contrary to one of the presuppositions of the free society. The function may be useful as a device in assisting the decision-making of a despot, benevolent or otherwise, an organic state, or a single-minded ruling group. But once this limitation is recognized, individual preferences, even as presumed by the observer, need not enter into the construction at all except in so far as it becomes necessary to consider predicted individual reaction to coercively-imposed changes. The Pareto conception of "optimality" loses most of its significance.

The approach adopted here is based upon the idea that no "social" values exist apart from individual values. Therefore, the political economist, instead of choosing arbitrarily some limited set of ethical norms for incorporation into a "social welfare function," searches rather for "social compromises" on particular issues. His proposals are hypotheses about individual values, hypotheses which are subjected to testing in the collective choice processes. Actual values are revealed only through the political action of individuals, and consensus among individual members of the choosing group becomes the only possible affirmation of a "social" value. The order which is present among "social" decisions, if indeed there is one, is revealed in the decision process itself, not external to it. Whereas the "social welfare function" approach searches for a criterion independent of the choice process itself, presumably with a view toward influencing the choice, the alternative approach evaluates results only in terms of the choice process itself.

VI. CONSENSUS AMONG REASONABLE MEN

In developing the argument of this essay, I have assumed that the social group is composed of reasonable men, capable of recognizing what they want, of acting on this recognition, and capable of being convinced of their own advantage after reasonable discussion. Governmental action, at the currently important margins of decision, is assumed to arise when such individuals agree that certain tasks should be collectively performed. To this extent, my argument rests on some implicit acceptance of a contract theory of the state.

I am aware of the limitations of this conception of society, and I can appreciate the force of the objection that may be raised on these grounds. Societies in the real world are not made up exclusively of reasonable men, and this fact introduces disturbing complications in any attempt to discuss the formation of social policy.

In outlining the structure of a possible non-evaluative political economy, I am suggesting that we proceed on an *as if* assumption. Despite our knowledge that some men are wholly unreasonable, we assume this away just as we have done in the organization of our whole democratic decision-making processes. In so far as "anti-social" or unreasonable individuals are members of the group, consensus, even where genuine "mutual gains" might be present, may be impossible. Here the absolute unanimity rule must be broken; the political economist must try, as best he can, to judge the extent of unanimity required to verify (not refute) his hypothesis. Some less definitive rule of relative unanimity must be substituted for full agreement, as Wicksell recognized and suggested.

This necessary modification does not materially reduce the strength of the argument presented. But it does place an additional responsibility upon the political economist. He is forced to discriminate between reasonable and unreasonable men in his search for consensus. This choice need not reflect the introduction of personal evaluation. Relatively objective standards may be adduced to aid in the discrimination process. Reflection from everyday experience with groups which use unanimity as the customary, but not essential, means of reaching decisions should reveal that the genuinely unreasonable individual can be readily identified. This reduction of the unanimity requirement to some relative unanimity does not suggest that "unreasonable" as a characteristic behavior pattern can be determined on the basis of one issue alone. And it should be emphasized that continuing disagreement with majority opinion suggests unreasonableness in no way whatsoever.

VII. MAJORITY RULE, CONSENSUS, AND DISCUSSION

The hypotheses which the political economist presents are tested by the measure of agreement reached, qualified only by the relative unanimity requirement introduced in the preceding section. But there remain two major practical difficulties to be confronted at this testing stage. These make the empirical testing difficult and, in some cases, impossible. First, collective decisions in democratically-organized societies may be, and normally are, made on the basis of some variant of majority rule rather than consensus or unanimity, even if the latter is qualified to rule out limited "anti-social" dissent.

The economist, employing his presumptive efficiency criterion, presents for consideration a policy change which embodies the hypothesis that the adoption of this change will constitute "improvement" in the "welfare" of the group in accordance with the Pareto rule. This proposal is then voted upon, either by all individuals in a referendum or by their representatives in a legislative body. If a majority rejects the proposal, the economist's hypothesis is clearly refuted, and alternatives must be sought. The hypothesis is equally refuted if a minority dissents, but the proposal may be carried on the basis of majority decision. This adoption tends to preclude the presentation of alternative hypotheses more acceptable to the minority. Majority rule, considered as a final means of making decisions, has the effect of closing off discussion and of thereby limiting severely the efforts of the political economist.

This result of majority rule places before the political economist a great temptation and also places upon him significant responsibility. Knowing that collective decisions are made by majority rule, he will be tempted to present social alternatives which may command majority support rather than consensus. Adequate compensations for damaged minorities may be omitted in the proposals suggested with a view toward making the majority more receptive. Deliberate attempts in this direction would violate the neutral position outlined for the political economist here, but given the inherently subjective basis for the presumptive efficiency criterion at best, the proposals presented may tend to reflect majority-oriented biases quite unintentionally. The danger that this bias will occur places upon the practitioner the responsibility of insuring that suggested proposals do, in fact, include compensations to damaged minorities estimated to be adequate, and, contrariwise, do not include overcompensations to damaged majorities.

The probability that decisions will be made without consensus being attained adds responsibility to the economist's task. Much greater care must be taken with the construction and application of the presumptive efficiency criterion. Again the analogy with the medical diagnostician may be helpful. Majority rule tends to place the political economist in the position of the diagnostician who may propose a fatal dosage if his diagnosis should prove incorrect. Hence he must be more careful than otherwise in proposing alternative remedies.

The practical difficulties introduced by majority rule may not be great if there exists consensus that all collective decisions reached in this way are temporary or provisional and are subject to reversal and modification. If majority rule is understood to be, not a means of making final decisions, but rather as one of making provisional choices while discussion continues, the possibility remains that alternative hypotheses can be presented subsequent to a favorable majority vote. No barrier to discussion need be introduced by majority rule conceived in this way.

But if majority rule is conceived as merely a step in the discussion process leading toward final agreement, a second major problem of practical importance arises. The whole process of discussion which characterizes the democratic idea implies that, in so far as concerns their behavior in making collective decisions, individuals do not have explicitly defined ends of an instrumental sort. If they do, discussion is bound to be fruitless, and an initial disagreement will persist. The purpose of political discussion is precisely that of changing "tastes" among social alternatives. The political economist, therefore, in constructing and applying his presumptive efficiency criterion, must try to incorporate the predicted preferences of individuals, not as they exist at a given moment, but as they will be modified after responsible discussion. In other words, he must try to predict "what reasonable individuals will reasonably want" after discussion, not what they "do want in a given moment" before discussion or what they "ought to want" if they agreed in all respects with the observer.

This recognition that individuals do not have *given ends* which can, at any moment, be taken as data by the observer appears to blur the sharp dividing line between "positive" political economy as here outlined and "normative" political economy which allows the observer to introduce his own ethical evaluations. This makes it more important that the attempt be made to test propositions in terms of expressed individual values instead of first attempting to estimate such values as a basis for decisions.

VIII. CONCLUSION

Positive science is concerned with the discovery of "what is," normative science with "what ought to be." Positive economics, narrowly conceived, overly restricts the "what is" category. Political economy has a non-normative role in discovering "what is the structure of individual values." The political economist, in accomplishing this task, can remain as free of personal value judgment as the positive economist. To be sure, the objectivity of the political economist is more difficult to preserve, and his behavior in departing from it more difficult for observers to detect. His hypotheses must take the form of policy propositions, and these may tend to appear as recommendations rather than hypotheses. And, since such hypotheses must be based on some presumptive efficiency criterion, an element of subjectivity is necessarily introduced. But the presence of subjective evaluation of the outside world (which includes the preference fields of other individuals) does not imply the infusion of an individual value judgment concerning the "goodness" of the proposal presented.

In a sense, the political economist is concerned with discovering "what people want." The content of his efforts may be reduced to very simple terms. This may be summed up in the familiar statement: *There exist mutual gains from trade.* His task is that of locating possible flaws in the existing social structure and in presenting possible "improvements." His specific hypothesis is that *mutual* gains do, in fact, exist as a result of possible changes (trades). This hypothesis is tested by the behavior of private people in response to the suggested alternatives. Since "social" values do not exist apart from individual values in a free society, consensus or unanimity (mutuality of gain) is the only test which can insure that a change is beneficial.

In his diagnosis and prescription, the economist must call upon all of the skills and resources which he possesses. These include the traditional "efficiency" tools, but in utilizing these he must beware of slipping into the easy assumption of omniscience. The individual preference patterns which he incorporates into his models must be conceived as presumed or predicted, and the changes which are based on these must always be considered tentative hypotheses to be subjected to testing in the polling places. The economist can never say that one social situation is more "efficient" than another. This judgment is beyond his range of competence. He presents a hypothesis that one situation is "presumed Pareto-efficient," and he allows the unanimity test (appropriately modified) to decide whether his prediction is correct or incorrect. From this it follows that all his proposals must embody estimated full compensations.

The role of the political economist as outlined here may be quite limited. This point would require considerable additional discussion. But beyond the area of "positive" political economy, there may be room for the individual to serve in a normative capacity as an especially well-informed citizen. Here his own ethical evaluations may be explicitly introduced, and he may choose to utilize certain welfare function constructions in this task.

Perhaps this essay may best be summarized by the consideration of a single example: the removal of a long-established tariff. The positive economist can predict that imports of the commodity will increase, that domestic prices of the commodity will fall, that exports will increase, that resources will be shifted from the domestic to the export industries, etc. The "positive" political economist, building on the fundamental theorems of positive economics, attempts to devise a proposal or proposals which will remove or reduce the tariff and be approved by an overwhelming majority of the whole social group. He advances a proposal which embodies a tariff reduction, along with estimated full compensation to the damaged industries financed out of a tax imposed on benefited groups. This proposal is advanced as a hypothesis. If the proposal is accepted by the whole group, the hypothesis is not refuted. If it is rejected, or approved by only a majority, the political economist should search for alternative schemes. In all of this, as an observer, he is ethically neutral. His own evaluations of the alternatives considered do not, and should not, influence his behavior in any way other than that necessarily arising out of his membership in the group.

If the reduction in the tariff, even when estimated full compensations are included, is not approved, the economist may, if he desires, discard his "scientific" cloak. He may introduce his own ethical evaluations and try to argue that a tariff reduction would be "good" for the whole group.

It seems useful that these three types of behavior of individuals calling themselves economists be separated and classified.

VI

THE METHODOLOGY OF INCIDENCE THEORY: A CRITICAL REVIEW OF SOME RECENT CONTRIBUTIONS*

DURING the last quarter-century, economists have devoted relatively little attention to the study of the pure theory of government finance in the classical or traditional sense. With few exceptions those interested in fiscal theory have concerned themselves with problems in the theory and application of fiscal (budgetary) policy in the post-Keynesian manner. They have tended to concentrate on the aggregative aspects of fiscal and monetary theory to the comparative neglect of theories of taxation and of public expenditure.

A shift back toward traditional theory is in order, and during the past few years, there have been indications that such a shift is in the process of taking place. A renewed interest in the theory of excise-tax incidence has been stimulated. Although independent developments of this interest have been evidenced, a substantial share of the credit must be attributed to Earl Rolph, whose work, represented by a series of articles,[1] and later in his book, *The*

* This essay represents a substantially modified version of a paper published in Italian: "La metodologia della teoria dell' incidenza," *Studi economici* (December, 1955). I have added the sections dealing with the Parravicini discussion, and I have changed the essay in a few other places.

1. Earl R. Rolph, "A Proposed Revision of Excise-Tax Theory," *Journal of Political Economy,* LX (1952), 102-17; "A Theory of Excise Subsidies," *American Economic Review,* XLII (1952), 515-27; "Government Burdens and Benefits: Discussion," *American Economic Review* XLIII (1953), 537-43; "A Theory of Excise Subsidies: Reply," *American Economic Review* XLIII (1953), 895-98.

Theory of Fiscal Economics,[2] has provoked a great deal of discussion and comment. Significant contributions to the debate have been made by John Due, R. A. Musgrave, H. P. B. Jenkins,[3] and G. Parravicini.

In this paper, I shall, first of all, review briefly the Rolph analysis. Secondly, I shall discuss the criticism of this analysis which is contained, implicitly or explicitly, in the other works mentioned. In the third, and substantive, portion of the paper I shall attempt to place the whole of the controversy into what I conceive to be the proper methodological setting.

I. ANALYSIS

Rolph's analysis consists in a refinement, extension, elaboration, and in some respects a substantial modification, of the theory first advanced in the United States by H. G. Brown.[4] The Brown thesis was that a genuinely general excise tax could not be shifted forward to consumers and, therefore, that the incidence of such a tax must rest on factor owners in proportion to factor incomes. In spite of the general validity of the argument, and its substantial acceptance in certain academic discussion,[5] the Brown thesis failed to gain widespread acceptance. Economists, trained in the Marshallian methodology, have tended to apply partial-equilibrium analysis to general excise taxation where it is, of course, inappropriate. The seldom-questioned conclusion that consumers tend to bear the incidence of general excise taxes stems from the

2. Berkeley: University of California Press, 1954.

3. John F. Due, "Toward a General Theory of Sales Tax Incidence," *Quarterly Journal of Economics,* LXVII (1953), 253-66; Richard A. Musgrave, "General Equilibrium Aspects of Incidence Theory," *American Economic Review,* XLIII (1953), 504-17; "On Incidence," *Journal of Political Economy,* LXI (1953), 306-23; H. P. B. Jenkins, "Excise-Tax Shifting and Incidence: A Money-Flows Approach," *Journal of Political Economy,* LXIII (1955), 125-49.

A critical note on the Rolph analysis has also been contributed by Lawrence Abbott: "A Theory of Excise Subsidies: Comment," *American Economic Review,* XLIII (1953), 890-95.

4. H. G. Brown, "The Incidence of a General Output or a General Sales Tax," *Journal of Political Economy,* XLVII (1939), 254-62.

5. Notably by the late Professor Henry C. Simons at the University of Chicago. Unfortunately the only published work by Simons on the issue is contained in an abstract of a paper delivered at the December, 1939, meeting of the American Economic Association. See *American Economic Review,* Supplement, XXX (1940), 242-44.

failure to recognize that the analyses of a partial excise tax and a general excise tax may require different theoretical frameworks.

Rolph deserves credit for having focused attention on this gap in existing fiscal theory in the United States. He attempted to go beyond the limits of the Brown analysis, however, and to extend the conclusions to apply to partial excises as well. At this point I shall try to outline the framework, procedure, and conclusions contained in Rolph's analysis.

Rolph analyzes the effects of a tax independently of changes in the level of government expenditures and/or other taxes. Both the level and composition of government expenditures and the level and structure of other taxes are thrown into the pound of *ceteris paribus.* He explicitly rejects the differential-incidence approach, which assumes offsetting variations in other taxes, or the balanced-budget approach, which assumes additional governmental spending to match the additional tax revenues.

The background of the Rolph approach to tax theory is to be found in the post-Keynesian emphasis upon taxes as tools of deflationary (anti-inflationary) policy and the consequent abandonment of budget equilibrium as a fiscal norm. If taxes are to be viewed primarily as deflationary, rather than as revenue-producing, devices in matters of budget policy, the application of this approach to incidence analysis appears to follow.

Closely connected with this underlying methodological assumption, and perhaps even more fundamental, is Rolph's definition of a tax. He defines a tax as a *money transfer payment* from the individual to the government. The long-cherished idea that taxes impose a *real* burden is labeled as a myth. The real burden from fiscal operations is held to arise from the expenditure not the tax side of the fiscal account. The aggregate real burden of government activity is determined solely by the share of total economic resources which the government commands. And, since Rolph impounds government expenditures in *ceteris paribus,* the aggregate real burden of government cannot change merely as the result of a tax change.

Explicit assumptions concerning the policies which are to be followed by the monetary authorities are somewhat strangely absent from Rolph's analysis. He fully recognizes the extreme importance of monetary theory in his version of incidence theory, and, at least in his book, he devotes considerable attention to the monetary basis of fiscal theory. But his monetary analysis is conducted almost entirely in terms of process. That is to say, he conceives monetary analysis to be completed by showing how a tax-induced deflation, for example, affects spendings decisions of individuals and firms. Nowhere does he specify the monetary framework within which the analysis is conducted. Rolph is, of course, not alone in this methodological omission. The failure to make explicit the type of monetary framework has weakened the efficacy of much, perhaps most, of the Keynesian analysis.[6]

The remaining characteristics of Rolph's analytical framework are more orthodox. These include the assumption of a fully competitive, closed economy in which resources are fully mobile in the long run. For analytical simplicity the simple two-commodity, no-saving model is used. While underlying assumptions of this general type have been, and may be, criticized as unduly limiting the applicability of the analysis, these will be accepted in the discussion of Section III.

We may now examine the procedural aspects of Rolph's analysis. He distinguishes sharply between the "income effect" of a tax and the "price-allocation" effect. The income effect is defined as the reduction in the money incomes of individuals made necessary by the levy of the tax. The tax, defined as a transfer payment, must reduce private money incomes and add to government income by equivalent amounts. In other words, the income effect of a tax must be exactly equal to the government's tax revenues. A tax may or may not generate, in addition, price-allocation effects in the economy.

Because of, and by way of, the income effect, a tax exerts a deflationary influence. Private spending power is lessened, and, by assumption, no offsetting inflationary effects are permitted to occur, either in additional government spending or in reduced

6. For an excellent recent statement on this point, see Fritz Machlup, "The Analysis of Devaluation," *American Economic Review,* XLV (1955), 273-75. Machlup says: "There has been a tendency in the 'New Economics' tacitly to regard the supply of money as a dependent variable rather than as a policy variable."

other taxes. The deflationary influence of the tax is, however, purely a monetary phenomenon. A tax imposes no real sacrifice. Those individuals and groups whose money incomes are reduced presumably bear the incidence of the tax.

These are shown to be all factor owners in the case of a truly general excise tax. The requirement that the tax be paid reduces the net price received by producing firms. Each firm will have an incentive to reduce output to the point at which marginal cost equals net price. But, since each firm is affected similarly, wholesale moves to limit output will create unemployment in factor markets. If factor markets are competitive, factor prices will fall enough to remove the unemployment. In the new equilibrium each firm will be producing as much as before the tax, and the net price will equal marginal cost. The adjustment will have been made solely through the lowered factor prices. Money incomes of factor owners are lower by the amount of the tax, and each individual bears the tax in proportion to the share of factor income which he receives. Since each firm continues to produce the same output as before the tax, the composition of output (the product-mix) will remain unchanged by the tax. The truly general excise tax (levied uniformly) on all products and services, has no price-allocation effects.

Rolph then extends this analysis to the case of partial excise taxation. Since the income effect must still be present, income receivers must still bear the tax load in the amount of the government's tax revenues. Supplementary price-allocation effects are present, however, in this case. The tax imposed on less-than-all goods and services, will tend to increase the price of the taxed goods relative to the untaxed.

Rolph reaches the following conclusions in his own words.

"(1) A system of completely general and uniform taxes leaves the composition of output unchanged, does not raise product prices, and reduces the money incomes of resource owners and does so proportionately.

"(2) Any partial system of excise taxes, . . . alters the product-mix, raises the prices of heavily taxed items, lowers the prices of lightly taxed and nontaxed items, and reduces the money incomes of resource owners.

"(3) All systems of excise taxation are deflationary. . . ."[7]

II. CRITICISM

It will be useful to review briefly the criticism of the Rolph analysis which has been advanced. It should be noted that each of the four treatments which I shall discuss here represents a general contribution to tax theory and is not limited to a criticism of the Rolph position. The common feature of the four, however, is the questioning of certain portions of Rolph's analysis. Therefore, the latter provides an appropriate unifying theme, at least for my purposes.

The Due Contribution

Due defines incidence in real terms. It is held to be the "pattern of the distribution of the burden of the tax; tax burden means the reduction in real income (. . .) which occurs as a result of the imposition of the tax."[8] His disagreement with Rolph is fundamental in that Rolph defines incidence in monetary terms and explicitly rejects the concept of "tax burden."

In his particular discussion of the Brown-Rolph case (which he treats as one), Due states that the validity of the conclusions rests upon three assumptions. These are: (1) Perfectly inelastic factor supplies, and a given quantity of money; (2) Perfect competition; and (3) Use of the tax revenue in such a manner that, taking into consideration both the tax and the use of the revenue, aggregate money demand for commodities remains unchanged.

As was mentioned above, the assumption of perfect competition was explicit in the Rolph analysis, and Due's criticism of the appropriateness of this assumption will not be discussed here. I tend to agree with Rolph that we must first clarify incidence theory in the simple cases before going on to the larger and more ambitious tasks. Assumption (3) appears to be implicit in Brown's analysis, which takes account of the government's use of revenues. But this is a point of distinction between Brown and Rolph. Rolph

7. "A Proposed Revision of Excise-Tax Theory," p. 102.
8. Due, *op. cit.*, p. 254.

explicitly impounds government spending in *ceteris paribus,* and emphasizes the deflationary effect of a tax. Due appears to overlook this distinction between Brown and Rolph. Due is correct in his comment that some of the Rolph conclusions will follow only on the assumption that aggregate demand is maintained. In his arithmetical models, Rolph uses a tax as an inflation-preventing device which, when superimposed on an inflationary gap situation, will act to keep aggregate demand, including tax supplements, equal to aggregate demand, excluding taxes, in the relevant preceding period. Presumably, if the tax had not been imposed, aggregate demand would have risen by the amount of the tax revenues, that is, inflation would have taken place. However, a careful reading of Rolph indicates that he considers his analysis to be equally applicable to all fiscal situations. And since he emphasizes the general deflationary effect of taxes, I think it may be surmised that if his conclusions depend on the maintenance of aggregate money demand, this is based on an error in his analysis rather than his failure to state his implicit assumptions.

Due tends to reject, by and large, the basic Rolph-Brown conclusion that general excise taxes are borne by factor owners rather than consumers, classifying this result as one possible situation out of many. Due's alternative explanation is based upon his assumption of an elastic money supply and the assumed failure of the monetary authorities to maintain stability in product prices. In his preferred framework, the tax-caused incentive to increase prices will be transmitted in actual price increases because aggregate money demand will be allowed to expand.

The Musgrave Contribution

Musgrave defines incidence as the changes which have occurred in the distribution of real income available for private use as a result of a tax.[9] He distinguishes three types of incidence which result alternatively from separate types of budgetary adjustment. First, a change in one tax with other taxes and public expenditures held constant is said to have an "absolute incidence." This is, of course, the Rolph framework. Secondly, one tax may be changed with corresponding and offsetting changes in a second

9. "On Incidence," *Journal of Political Economy,* LXI (1953), 306.

tax, thus keeping total government revenue constant. The distributional result of these changes is classified as "differential incidence." Finally, a tax may be changed along with the corresponding changes in public expenditures. The result is called "balanced-budget incidence." Musgrave argues persuasively for the "differential incidence" approach to fiscal theory, but he accepts each of the three approaches as methodologically permissible.

Musgrave's analysis, which is conducted solely in differential and balanced-budget terms, demonstrates that the particular monetary framework which is postulated becomes all important in determining the direction of adjustment in absolute prices which are occasioned by a tax change. Different conclusions follow, depending upon whether a policy of constant money supply, constant price level, or some other alternative is initially assumed. He attempts to show, however, that the direction of adjustment in absolute prices, or the price level, has no effect on the incidence pattern. The direction of adjustment in absolute prices is a purely monetary phenomenon which does not affect the distribution of the tax burden. "The theory of incidence is inherently a theory of relative prices, while monetary manipulations in this setting bear on the price level only."[10]

Musgrave recognizes two fallacies inherent in the traditional analytical route by which the conclusion that consumers bear general excise taxes on consumer goods has been reached. He gives credit to both Brown and Rolph for discovering one of the fallacies, that is, the idea that individual firm adjustments may allow prices to rise. But he accuses them of having failed to escape from the second fallacy. This is the fallacy of confusing the direction of adjustment in absolute prices with tax incidence. By showing that, under certain conditions, factor prices fall by the amount of the tax, Musgrave argues that Brown and Rolph have not shown that factor owners bear the tax. Musgrave shows that the incidence pattern may be identical even if the direction of adjustment is such as to cause the level of prices to increase, to decrease, or to remain unchanged.

Following his discussion of the consumption economy, Musgrave considers an economy with both consumption goods and

10. *Ibid.*, p. 314.

capital goods. Introducing a tax on consumption goods, he shows that the prices of capital goods are reduced relative to those of consumer goods, and that the real incidence of the tax depends on the individual purchase pattern between consumption and capital goods. Here his treatment differs from that of Rolph or of Jenkins precisely in that he introduces capital goods.

Following this analysis of a general excise tax on consumer goods (which is not a general excise tax in the Brown-Rolph sense), Musgrave examines the tax imposed generally and uniformly on all capital goods while consumer goods are left untaxed. He concludes that such a tax will be borne exclusively by the suppliers of savings. He arrives at this result by sharply separating the production of consumer goods from that of capital goods, the former being produced by direct labor and previously-produced capital goods, the latter by direct labor and "waiting." Having analyzed the incidence of a general tax on consumer goods and a general tax on capital goods, Musgrave then proceeds to combine these two in his analysis of the genuinely general excise tax. Since the tax on capital goods is supposedly borne by the suppliers of savings, the tax falling on consumer goods must be exclusively borne by consumers if the general excise tax is to be equivalent in incidence to a general income tax on factor returns (the Brown-Rolph conclusion). Consumers bear the full burden of the consumer goods excise tax only if all wage income is used in consumption and all interest income is saved. Since these requirements are unrealistic, Musgrave concludes that the general Rolph proposition does not hold except in the rarified all-consumption model.

Musgrave's analysis appears unchallengeable, in large part, if one is willing to accept the underlying theory of capital upon which it is based. He accepts, without qualification, the Austrian theory of capital in which capital goods represent "produced" means of production. His sharp conceptual separation between the capital goods and the consumer goods sector of the economy seems possible only on the basis of this capital theory. If, on the other hand, one rejects the Austrian theory and substitutes for it the Knightian formulation, the Musgrave analysis will not be correct. The distinctive separation between consumer goods production and capital goods production disappears, and the conclusions reached on the assumption of an all-consumption goods model will be unchanged by the introduction of capital goods into the picture, at least in the static analysis.

The Jenkins Contribution

I shall now discuss contributions to the excise-tax incidence controversy made by H. P. B. Jenkins. His analysis is exceedingly complex, and it is difficult to discuss outside the framework of his arithmetical analytical models. However, a summary of his procedures and his conclusions may be attempted.

Jenkins' technique consists in tracing the pattern of incidence through the effects of the tax on money flow. Although his particular analysis is framed in differential-incidence terms, he argues that his conclusions follow regardless of the assumptions made concerning the level of government expenditures, other taxes, and monetary policy. Explicit assumptions concerning these three policy variables are useful for analytical clarity and convenience only, according to Jenkins, since they affect only the absolute sizes of the money flow.

Jenkins argues that Rolph confuses monetary deflation with tax shifting. On this point he and Musgrave are in agreement. But Jenkins also criticizes Musgrave and says that the latter does not distinguish properly between the false and true incidence of taxes. Jenkins defines incidence as "the pattern in which the imputed retail product value of the state-supplied (services) is imbedded in the structure of final market payments."[11] In the sense that this definition is essentially monetary, Jenkins' conception of incidence would appear to be more closely akin to that of Rolph than to either Musgrave or Due. This affinity is, however, more apparent than real, for, in spite of the monetary definition, Jenkins' analysis of incidence is essentially in real terms.

Rolph argues that the income effects of a tax, which he does not explicitly label as "incidence" but seems to imply as a preferred definition, can be no greater than the government's tax take; and the price-allocation effects, if they are present, must be supple-

11. Jenkins, *op. cit.*, p. 131.

mentary to this primary magnitude. Jenkins argues in a somewhat similar fashion that the genuine or true monetary value of the tax load cannot exceed the imputed value of the government purchases of goods and services. The real income reductions supplementary to this, which are occasioned by a tax, cannot be true incidence. He calls them false incidence, or, more specifically, horizontal shifts in retail product-value. Musgrave includes both Jenkins' "true" incidence and these shifts in product-value in his broader definition.

Jenkins' analysis specifically includes the consideration of the government sector of the economy, and he criticizes both Rolph and Musgrave for their failure to examine carefully the purchases made by government. First of all, Jenkins shows that for a tax to be truly general in effect it must be extended to government purchases as well as to all private purchases. In this case, the Brown-Rolph conclusion of full backward shifting holds; the full incidence of the tax rests on the owners of resources. However, if the tax is not extended to include the government's purchases, but is instead limited to the private sector, the analysis reveals that, except in the production subsidy case where there is complete forward shifting, the tax will be partially borne by factor owners and partially by consumers.

He shows that the money value of the tax load upon factor owners in the case when all goods except government purchases are taxed will always be equal to the government's excise tax revenue. This supports the initial Rolph conclusion. But he holds Rolph to be in error in stopping at this point. Jenkins' analysis demonstrates that there exists an additional burden imposed on consumers over and above the money value of the government's tax take. This additional or supplementary burden is always in proportion to the amount shifted backward, with the ratio dependent on the size of the total tax load in the economy.

For analytical convenience, Jenkins assumes that the tax under alternative models remains just sufficient to finance a given amount of government purchases in real terms. It is quite easy to measure the proportion of the productive factors of the economy which go into producing the government-purchased goods. In his models the proportion is always one-fifth. This suggests that four-fifths of the productive effort of the economy goes into the production of privately-purchased goods and services. This provides Jenkins with a benchmark from which the position of consumers may be measured. If consumers of privately-purchased goods and services are found to give up more than four-fifths of total retail product values in the purchase of the taxed goods, the excess over and above four-fifths is a part of the tax load, and is borne by consumers. In effect, this analysis says that because factor prices are reduced somewhat, and government purchases are not taxable, the government is getting a "bargain" in its purchases. This distortion in the structure of payments makes the real tax load greater than the apparent load which is limited to the tax revenues.

Jenkins' disagreement with Musgrave is more subtle, and it appears only in the analysis of the partial excise tax. As mentioned earlier, it stems from a slight difference in the definition of incidence. The Jenkins benchmark for measuring money burden on consumers is the share of factor costs implicit in the production of consumer goods. The share of total retail purchase payments which is over and above this share of factor costs provides a measure of excess burden on consumers. But his analysis reveals that, when an excise tax is levied on a single commodity (or less than all commodities) the amount paid out in retail product value by consumers of the taxed good over and above "imputed retail price" exceeds the true incidence of the tax. Tax incidence, to Jenkins, it should be recalled, is itself composed of two components, the government's tax take plus the additional retail value of the real incidence on consumers. But there is still a further amount over and above this paid out by the consumers of the taxed commodity in the partial excise tax case. There is an additional or supplementary shifting of retail product value which is occasioned by the imposition of the tax. Jenkins holds Musgrave to be in error for including this in tax incidence.

The way in which this supplementary shifting in retail product value arises may be shown briefly. A tax on a single good reduces costs of all other goods and services. Thus, consumers of non-taxed goods and services actually secure a positive benefit from the levy of the excise tax just as the government does in the general excise and the partial excise tax case. But consumers of non-taxed goods secure this benefit at the expense of the consumers of the taxed good. To add this "burden," which is borne by consumers of the taxed good to offset the "benefits" gained by other consumers, in with tax incidence is illegitimate, according to Jenkins. The change in the relative prices of the taxed commodities overstates the amount of true tax incidence falling on consumers of the taxed commodity. The amount of the differential which is offset by the concealed subsidy to other consumers is a mere shifting which the consumers of the taxed items may always escape by consuming taxed and non-taxed items in the same ratio as the average or representative man.

The Parravicini Contribution

Giannino Parravicini has represented Italy in this incidence debate.[12] His argument, developed independently as a critique of the Brown-Rolph thesis, contains elements which are similar in some respects to the arguments of both Musgrave and Jenkins. The closest affinity is to the discussion of Due, however, although Parravicini's treatment is somewhat more sophisticated.

He postulates, as a condition of his model, constancy in the quantity of money and in the circuit velocity of money. He then demonstrates that the imposition of the excise tax must act so as to increase the income velocity of money. This effect is exerted through the reduction in the "work load" of money which the tax-spending operation accomplishes. The general excise tax, levied normally on the final stage of distribution, channels funds through a fiscal income circuit which contains fewer vertical stages than the more normal private income circuit. If, therefore, both the quantity of money and the circuit velocity are held constant, the effect of the general excise tax must be a general rise in prices.

12. Giannino Parravicini, "Imposte indirette su merce e livello generale dei prezzi," *Moneta e credito* (1954), 144-64; 298-312; "Imposte, moneta, e prezzi," *Rivista di diritto finanziario e scienza delle finanze,* XV (1956), 111-36.

III. COMMENT

The preceding discussion of the various contributions to incidence theory has been too concise to convey the many subtleties and complexities of the separate analyses. I have done nothing more than attempt to convey what appears to me to be the major contributions of each participant. Some of the points which remain obscure may be clarified in this section in which my own ideas on the debate are developed.

The issues in the debate appear to be fundamentally methodological rather than analytical. Some issues of a methodological nature may be resolved into questions of choice. The existing differences between the analyses of Brown, Musgrave, and Jenkins can be reduced to differences in their choice of definitions and non-fiscal presuppositions. The conclusions of both Due and Parravicini, on the other hand, depend strictly upon the monetary framework which they assume as relevant for analysis. But methodological errors may also be made, and this whole incidence debate is characterized by such an error on the part of Rolph, and the subsequent failure of his critics to make this error explicit although each of them appears to have recognized its presence.[13]

In the discussion which follows I hope to be able to support the following propositions:

1. The Brown-Rolph conclusion that a genuinely general excise tax is shifted backward and that the incidence rests upon the owners of productive resources is substantially correct.

2. Rolph is in error when he states that such a tax will not alter the product-mix, while Brown, within the limited context of his analysis, is careful and correct in his statements on this point.

3. A partial excise tax will tend normally to be borne by both resource owners and consumers of the taxed commodity, with the larger share of the total burden normally borne by resource owners.

4. Rolph commits his fundamental methodological error when he attempts to analyze a tax independently. His error is one of the

13. It is most clearly seen by Abbott, but he does not frame the issue in its most general terms. Abbott, *op. cit.*

more basic type which involves an improper usage of the economist's tool of *ceteris paribus.*

5. Any tax must impose a real burden since any tax which fails to impose such a burden would be functionally useless.

6. The difference between Musgrave and Jenkins may be explained by a clarification of the implied nature of a tax in each of their analyses.

7. The Jenkins conception of a tax is more in keeping with traditional usage, and it does serve to sharpen the tools of incidence theory. But the Musgrave conception, if properly employed, may be extended more generally and is therefore methodologically superior for some purposes.

8. The most appropriate monetary assumption for incidence theory is governmental action to stabilize some index of final product prices. Only with the aid of this assumption can the incidence of the tax be conceptually isolated from the incidence of monetary policy.

Since the above propositions are not unrelated, the discussion of each of them will not be independent. It will be useful, however, to use these propositions as a convenient outline.

1. There seems to be widespread agreement that the Brown-Rolph conclusions concerning the incidence of a completely general excise tax are correct. Even if prices are allowed to go up by the amount of the uniform tax, as in Due's inflationary model, resource owners are still made worse off relative to non-resource owners assuming that the inflation would have occurred without the tax. And surely we should not attribute the inflationary policies of the monetary authorities to the tax. Musgrave accepts the equivalence between the general products tax and the income tax on factor incomes in his all-consumption model; and, as we have indicated, with an alternative capital theory, the all-consumption model becomes the general framework for analysis in comparative statics. This is, of course, not the place to enter into a discussion of the profound and still largely unexplored regions of capital theory, but I should go on record as stating my preference for the Knightian theory, which is implicit in the Rolph analysis. Jenkins agrees with the Rolph conclusion in the case where taxes are ex-

tended to government-purchased goods as well as to those privately purchased. In this particular respect, Jenkins' contribution lies in his showing that a tax is not general unless the government purchases are included.

The controversy over analytical fine points and over methodology, no matter how important these may be, should not be allowed to obscure the fundamental agreement which exists on the location of the incidence of general excise taxes. There has been and continues to be, an all-too-facile extension of partial equilibrium tools to situations where they will not work, and if used, will lead to wrong conclusions. And even should economists all become sophisticated in this respect, the tremendous need for the education of the mildly sophisticated policy-making groups in society should not be overlooked. Journalists and politicians need to learn that the difference between a general excise tax, or a whole set of partial excises, and a proportional income tax is slight indeed.

2. Each of the participants in the recent debate with the exception of Jenkins, and including Rolph himself, seems to have overlooked the fact that there is a basic difference between the Brown analysis and the Rolph analysis of general excise taxes. The difference is that the Brown analysis is admittedly framed in terms of balanced-budget incidence, with particular attention given to the government's securing and the spending of the newly collected tax revenues. Brown explicitly recognizes that, as a result of the tax, the government will have more to spend and the individual will have less to spend. "Individually, the people have less money to spend. Collectively—*through the sales tax receipts,* to be spent by government—they have more to spend."[14] This causes Brown to be very careful when he implies that the composition of output will be unchanged as a result of the tax. While a hasty reading may indicate that he considered the composition of output to remain unaltered, he specifically recognizes in a footnote that if the pattern of government demand is different from that of private demand this conclusion will not hold.[15] It is interesting

14. Brown, *op. cit.,* p. 259.

15. "Of course, less individual spending and more collective spending might change the relative demands for and marginal cost of various kinds of goods and so have some effects on their relative prices." *Ibid.,* p. 260.

to note that Rolph, in referring to Brown's analysis, recognizes the differential incidence aspects contained in it, but that he fails to see that the tentative Brown conclusion on the product-mix depends for its partial validity strictly on this assumed framework.[16] If the offsetting variation in either government expenditures or other taxes is ruled out, the imposition of a general excise tax must set in motion forces which will alter the composition of output.

This may be shown in the following manner. Suppose that a general excise tax is levied on all goods and services, with government collections of other taxes in money and government expenditures in money remaining unchanged. (These are the Rolph assumptions.) The government must be assumed to hoard the revenues collected although Rolph nowhere makes the necessity of this step explicit. The tax collection will exert a deflationary impact on the economy; the incomes of factor owners will be reduced, the incomes of certain groups and of government from other sources will remain unchanged (in money terms). In so far as the demand pattern of the latter two diverges from the demand pattern of resource owners the product-mix must be modified.

Under any other conditions in which the new tax is substituted for an old, or in which the newly collected revenues are used to finance additional government purchases, the product-mix will clearly be altered as a result of the fiscal process.

3. Perhaps the major contribution of Rolph lies in his extension of the analysis of general excise taxes to partial excise taxes, and his demonstration that a portion of the incidence of partial excise taxes rests on factor owners rather than upon consumers of the taxed goods. The Brown analysis did not contain this extension, and the partial-equilibrium conclusions have been almost universally applied in the case of partial excises. For some purposes, partial-equilibrium analysis remains appropriate, but the

16. "According to the Brown theory, a general system of excise taxation leaves the composition of output and product prices absolutely and relatively unchanged *as compared with a system of taxation of equal yield having zero announcement effects in Pigou's sense.*" "A Proposed Revision of Excise-Tax Theory," *Journal of Political Economy*, LX (1952), 107 (Italics mine).

general-equilibrium framework is always conceptually more correct. The partial-equilibrium emphasis appears to have been due to the concentrated incidence on consumers brought about by the increase in the prices of taxed goods relative to untaxed goods. Jenkins' analysis is extremely helpful in isolating the relative shares borne by factor owners and consumers in the partial excise tax model.

4. Rolph commits a fundamental methodological error when he attempts to analyze a new tax independently of change either in other taxes or in public expenditures and fails to follow through to the full consequences of the tax-induced monetary deflation. He argues that it is entirely legitimate to throw both public expenditures and other taxes into *ceteris paribus* and to analyze the effect of a tax as such. If this approach is taken, however, full account must be taken of the deflationary effects of the tax. Monetary conditions cannot be thrown into *ceteris paribus,* explicitly or implicitly. When Rolph proceeds to throw all the possible offsetting effects into *ceteris paribus,* either explicitly or through neglect, he is using this tool, which has been extremely helpful to economists and which can continue to be of great assistance if employed properly, in an entirely wrong way. We may legitimately throw into *ceteris paribus* those variables which are either entirely unaffected by the movement of the variable upon which our analysis acts or, if affected, vary to such slight degree that the assumption of constancy does not invalidate our conclusions. But it is illegitimate to assume as constant things which, by the very nature of our analytical operation, must vary, that is, to assume as constants those magnitudes which must co-vary with the action variable. In price theory, we modify one price and examine its effects on the *ceteris paribus* assumption that money income does not change. We may do this because a change in one price does not appreciably change money income. If, however, we were studying an institutional setting in which wage rates were tied to a single price, we could not employ this usual assumption of money income constancy when examining the demand for the bellwether commodity. Or, to take an example from outside economics, suppose that we wish to analyze the effects of drawing down the water level in a

reservoir. It may be useful to impound such things as rainfall, temperature, etc. in *ceteris paribus,* but we cannot include in this the water level of all other receptacles in the relevant watershed. This appears to be what Rolph attempts to do. He tries to analyze the effects of a tax, without tracing through the necessary offsetting effects. Of course, it is a matter of choice which of three routes is to be selected. One may select the other-tax reduction route which Musgrave prefers. Or the balanced-budget method may be used. Or, if one chooses, he may impose a tax change, change neither government expenditures nor other taxes, and trace through the full effects of the monetary deflation which results. Had Rolph done this, his analysis would have been vastly improved. The latter choice, however, would seem the least appropriate of the three. But the important point here is that *one* of the three must be selected, and when this is admitted, the concept of absolute incidence in the larger sense must be ruled out of court. Offsetting changes in other variables must be present. All that the analyst may do is to choose which of the offsetting variables he wishes to allow to move.

In fairness to Rolph on this point it should be noted that he is by no means alone in the misuse of *ceteris paribus.* The malady is quite common among economists, and it is especially prevalent among those who have accepted and utilized the Hicksian version of the Marshallian demand curve. The methodological contribution of Milton Friedman on this subject is essentially that of showing how the assumptions underlying the orthodox demand curve are mutually inconsistent, that is, how they imply a misuse of *ceteris paribus,* and will lead to erroneous analytical results.[17]

5. Rolph defines a tax as a monetary phenomenon, a transfer payment from the individual to the government. As such it is

17. Milton Friedman, "The Marshallian Demand Curve," *Journal of Political Economy,* LVII (1949), 463-95; "The 'Welfare' Effects of an Income Tax and an Excise Tax," *Journal of Political Economy,* LX (1952), 25-33. See also his essay, "The Methodology of Positive Economics," contained along with the other two essays in *Essays in Positive Economics* (Chicago: University of Chicago Press, 1953).

For a general discussion of the use of *ceteris paribus,* see my "Ceteris Paribus: Some Notes on Methodology," *Southern Economic Journal,* XXIV (1958), 259-70.

held not to impose a real burden. This represents a radical departure from orthodoxy in fiscal theory, and it warrants careful consideration. Since a tax may be used purely as an inflation-preventing device, having no connection with the level of public expenditures, Rolph prefers to analyze a tax in this purely monetary role. This is, of course, perfectly *proper.* But again certain methodological rules of the game must be observed.

Let us look at his example of the tax which imposes no real burden. It is a tax which is levied for the sole purpose of preventing inflation and which succeeds in accomplishing this purpose.[18] Product prices, on the average, are the same before and after the tax. The same total of real goods is produced for private uses since the government's usage of resources is not modified by the tax. It is easy to see how the conclusion that such a tax imposes no real burden is reached. But it is here that Rolph's time-period analysis becomes treacherous and creates difficulties. Relative positions of individuals before and after the tax may be identical. But the proper comparison is not *before* and *after.* Rather it is *without the tax* and *with the tax.* In normal economic analysis, which starts from positions of equilibria, this distinction is not important. But if the analysis begins from a dis-equilibrium position, it is important and necessary. If the imposition of a tax succeeds in just preventing inflation which *would otherwise have occurred,* quite obviously the initial position is a dis-equilibrium one. In this case, the effects of the tax must be compared with the effects of the inflation which would have taken place in the absence of the tax. Static analysis must always compare alternative positions at the same instant of time, not successive positions over time. It is apparent that, if the tax is compared in effect with the inflation, there is a very real burden connected with its imposition. Those individuals and groups who *would have benefited by the inflation* are subjected to a real burden as a result of the tax. Those groups who would have been harmed are the offsetting beneficiaries. In an all-inclusive sense, inflation can best be looked upon as a tax of sorts, and Rolph's analysis becomes one of differential incidence after all.

18. Rolph, "Government Burdens and Benefits: Comment," *American Economic Review,* XLIII (1953), 539.

But need a tax levied solely to prevent inflation impose real burdens on some groups and benefit other groups in the sense outlined above? Is a real burden on some individuals a necessary result of the levy of such a tax? The initial answer would appear to be in the negative. It is conceptually possible that the tax could be levied in such a fashion that it would fall on precisely those individuals who would be harmed by the inflation, and precisely in proportion to their real burdens under the inflation. This would put all individuals in exactly the same relative position as they *would have been* had the inflation been allowed to occur. This is, however, only a conceptual possibility, for no government would ever impose such a tax. And we do not need to rely on the political impracticability of such a tax to demonstrate this point. Such a tax would be *functionally useless.* If the purpose of the tax is to prevent inflation, it would succeed. Therefore, it would appear to have some function. But we must go behind this to the government's desire to prevent inflation. If individuals and groups are to be left in the same relative positions which they would be in if the inflation occurs, what possible interest could the government have in preventing the inflation? Inflation is undesirable because it does redistribute incomes, and because it does so in an undesirable way. If inflation did not do this, it is hard to see why government need be concerned about the level of absolute prices at all. From this it may be concluded that even a purely inflation-preventing tax must impose a real burden on some individuals and groups. To be sure the real burden is, wholly or partially, offset by real benefits, but this is no different from taxes imposed to finance new government services.

Rolph would perhaps accept the argument of the preceding paragraph. He admits that such a tax may redistribute incomes. But he is led to conclude that no real burden is imposed by his concentration on the aggregative aspects. If the amount of real resources available for private purposes does not change, can the community be said to undergo a real burden? To say that it does not, but that redistribution does occur, is to say that one may compare utilities among individuals. In so far as redistribution takes place, the real burdens imposed on losers may exceed or fall short of the real benefits conferred on the gainers. Only on the assumption that dollar changes in income in either direction affect all individuals identically can the idea of no real aggregate burden be supported. We may conclude, therefore, that the orthodox idea that all taxes do impose real burdens has not been so badly shaken by the Rolph attack.

6. Although neither of them makes his implied definition of a tax explicit, I believe that the analyses of both Musgrave and Jenkins may be clarified if we attempt to "read into" their treatment such definitions. Musgrave "should" define a tax as "a transfer of command over the disposal of real resources away from the individual or individuals" which is occasioned by the fiscal activity of government. Jenkins "should" define a tax as "a transfer of command over the disposal of real resources away from the individual or individuals *to government*" which is occasioned by the fiscal activity of government. Note that these definitions are identical except for the words "to government" which are added to the implied Musgrave definition in the Jenkins definition. This difference will allow Musgrave to include the horizontal shifting of retail product values which has been isolated by the Jenkins analysis in tax incidence. The Jenkins definition would exclude these from incidence, and allow him to label these burdens as "false incidence." Of course, it should be noted that if the suggested Musgrave conception of a tax is accepted, which includes the reduction in real incomes occasioned by the tax even if the reductions amount to transfers among individuals which are not channeled through government, a corresponding conception of government benefits should also be accepted. If taxes are defined to include the horizontal shifts in retail product value, government benefits must be defined to include those accruing to the recipients of these transfers.

7. The question remains to determine which of the two imputed conceptions of a tax is the most useful. (It should be emphasized that both are "imputed" to the writers in question as implications of their analyses. Each might, of course, reject the definition here imputed to him.) The Jenkins conception is clearly more in keeping with orthodox fiscal theory. The transfers of

real income among individuals or groups, even if occasioned by the fiscal actions of government, have seldom been included in taxes or in benefits. For many purposes, this should remain the appropriate construction. It does allow, as Jenkins' analysis demonstrates, a sharp separation to be made between the real resources given up to government and to other groups as a result of the imposition of a tax. It should lead to better results when the purpose is to study the "efficiency" of the over-all tax system.

But the Jenkins conception appears somewhat deficient when one attempts to extend the analysis to situations such as that posited by Rolph. If the tax is purely monetary, that is, if it just succeeds in preventing inflation, no real resources are transferred to government. The real income transfers which are caused by the tax are solely among individuals and groups and are accomplished without real resources being channeled through the fisc. If the Jenkins analysis is extended to apply specifically to the Rolph case above, it is necessary to adopt the Musgrave variant of the tax. The Jenkins conception works well when we remain in the realm of differential or balanced-budget incidence. I think that there are many good reasons why we should keep fiscal theory within these confines and not introduce all of monetary theory into the analysis. But in so far as some analysts attempt to go beyond these more orthodox boundaries, the "Musgrave" conception of a tax does provide a useful methodological tool. Under it we may take any conceivable fiscal operation, examine its effects, label those that reduce individuals' real income "taxes" and those that increase individuals' real income "benefits." In so doing, we sacrifice some of the analytical sharpness that is present in the Jenkins version, but the added ability to deal with all cases may be worth the sacrifice.

In summary it is well that we have the two concepts. Both are useful and the analyst must, as always, choose the tools appropriate to his particular task.

8. Much of the recent discussion could have been greatly clarified if the participants had taken care to define explicitly the monetary framework within which the analysis is to be conducted. There is, of course, no single specific monetary assumption which

is "correct." The problem is one of choice, and the monetary framework chosen should not affect the conclusion reached on tax incidence. Nevertheless, the fact that much of the dispute has arisen over the failure to distinguish between tax incidence and "monetary policy incidence" indicates that there do exist "better" and "worse" monetary asumptions.

In my opinion, there is a strong argument for assuming at the outset of analysis that the monetary authorities are successful in enforcing a rule which guarantees over-all stability in the appropriately defined index of final product prices. This monetary assumption may be defended on grounds of economy; it eliminates all need for considering any incidence of general price inflation or deflation along with the problem of separating such incidence from tax incidence per se. The reductions in real income which result from the imposition of a general sales or excise tax in this model make up a pattern of tax incidence. And it becomes quite clear that the "wedge" between product prices and factor prices is inserted by the shifting downward of the latter. This conclusion holds whether the necessary compensating variation takes the form of increased public spending, decreased "other" taxes, or neutralization of the proceeds of the tax. In each case, individual factor owners are placed in a relatively worsened position as a result of the excise tax, relative to their position prevailing if all other things, including the individualized shares of the compensating variation, were to remain unchanged by the removal of the excise. In either of these fiscal models which combine a general excise tax on the one side and some appropriate compensating variation on the other, some supplementary monetary-fiscal action may be necessary to maintain price-level stability. But the effects of such supplementary action should be sharply distinguished from the effects of the tax levy.

The advantages of this monetary assumption suggested here may be indicated by a contrast with the models of Due and Parravicini. Due explicitly accepts a framework in which the monetary authorities respond to tax-induced attempts to increase product prices by either expanding the supply of money or acquiescing in the price increases which the tax-caused economizing of currency allows. This model leads him to conclude that since the general excise tax does result in an increase in the absolute level of product prices, consumers may be said to "bear" the "burden" of the tax. The effective incidence of the tax becomes dependent upon the sort of monetary policy which is assumed. Clearly, there is a failure here to examine relevant alternatives for comparison. If the same degree of product-price inflation is assumed to take place with or without the tax, then it becomes clear that factor owners are placed in a less favorable position with the tax than without it. The incidence pattern remains the same as under the other monetary assumptions.

Parravicini assumes a monetary framework in which both the quantity of money and the circuit velocity of money are fixed. His argument reduces to showing that the general excise tax increases the level of product prices owing to the greater economy in the use of money which the tax facilitates. There is considerable precedent for the fixed quantity assumption in economic models, and, to a certain extent, the attributing of the price level increase to the tax is legitimate. However, it seems preferable, even in this case, to attribute the over-all price level increase (if it occurs) to monetary policy and to isolate the incidence of price inflation from that of the tax levy. Only in this way can the pattern of tax incidence be made fully independent of the monetary framework postulated.

The analysis of Due, and also Parravicini to a certain extent, is equivalent to that which has recently been advanced in other connections. The so-called "cost or wage-push" explanations of price inflation, by placing the cause of inflation on cost-price increases, assume elasticity in the money supply. The opponents of this view argue that the cause of price inflation is the expansion in the money supply itself and not the cost-push elements. The choice between these two approaches depends, I suspect, upon the sort of "monetary rules" implicit in the analyst's conception of the "good society." The "cost-push" proponents (or the Due version of excise tax incidence) picture the economic good society as one in which there is considerable elasticity in the money supply and/or considerable short-run variability in income velocity.

The general product price level is, therefore, a dependent variable even in the "ideal" system. On the other hand, the advocates of the opposing view, which has somewhat erroneously been called the "Chicago school," conceive the economic good society as one in which either clearly defined rules, a fully automatic standard, or omniscient discretionary authorities, act so as to stabilize the level of either final product or factor prices. "Neutral money," at least in this sense, must be a meaningful conception. The absolute price level is a variable which is appropriately subjected to control; it becomes a controlled rather than a dependent variable.

IV. CONCLUSION

The recent debate on the incidence of general excise taxes is not concluded. Many questions, some of which are analytical and some of which are methodological, remain to be clarified. The discussion reflects a larger development in economic theory generally, the application of the theory of general equilibrium to problems which have previously been attacked, and improperly, only with partial-equilibrium weapons.

VII

COMPARATIVE TAX ANALYSIS AND ECONOMIC METHODOLOGY*

THE comparison of the effects of direct and indirect taxation has long been a favorite topic in fiscal theory. Barone was apparently the first to apply the modern indifference-opportunity tools of analysis and to arrive at the now familiar conclusion concerning the "excess burden" of the partial excise tax over the income tax of equal yield levied on the individual.[1] Barone's work was followed in Italy by Borgatta,[2] and the analysis was more fully developed by Fasiani.[3] Some years later the argument appeared in English in the celebrated note by Miss Joseph,[4] and it has since been repeated many times.[5]

Three important recent articles[6] have sharply criticized the

* I am indebted to Professors Milton Friedman and Warren Nutter for helpful comments and suggestions.

1. E. Barone, "Studi di economia finanziaria," *Giornale degli economisti* (1912), II, 329-30 in notes.

2. G. Borgatta, "Intorno alla pressione di qualunque imposta a parità di prelievo," *Giornale degli economisti* (1929), II, 290-97.

3. M. Fasiani, "Di un particolare aspetto delle imposte sul consumo," *La riforma sociale,* XL (1930), 1-20.

4. M. F. W. Joseph, "The Excess Burden of Indirect Taxation," *Review of Economic Studies,* VI (1938-1939), 226-31.

5. For a listing of other references see, David Walker, "The Direct-Indirect Tax Problem: Fifteen Years of Controversy," *Public Finance,* II (1955), 153-76.

6. Earl R. Rolph and George F. Break, "The Welfare Aspects of Excise Taxes," *Journal of Political Economy,* LVII (1949), 46-54; I. M. D. Little, "Direct versus Indirect Taxation," *Economic Journal,* LXI (1951), 577-84; Milton Friedman, "The 'Welfare' Aspects of an Income Tax and an Excise Tax," *Journal of Political Economy,* LX (1952), 25-33, reprinted in *Essays in Positive Economics* (Chicago: University of Chicago Press, 1953), pp. 100-16. Subsequent references will be to the latter.

excess burden analysis and have developed an alternative analytical approach to the problem. Friedman argues that the excess burden analysis illustrates a fruitless methodological approach to economic theory in general.

This paper attempts to synthesize the two approaches. As such, its purpose is as much methodological as analytical. I shall refer to the first approach as the Barone analysis, giving some credit to its originator.[7] I shall refer to the second approach as the production-possibility analysis. My argument will fully support the criticism of the recent papers to the application of the Barone analysis to general welfare problems. However, I shall demonstrate that the proposed alternative analytical construction is not fully acceptable. In its most restricted form the production-possibility model will be shown to contain assumptions which severely limit its applicability to real-world problems. The compression of the model which is necessary to eliminate the existence of all differential production-possibility or income effects of the excise tax renders the model rather barren of content, but, somewhat interestingly, such compression largely removes the ambiguity from conclusions about general welfare. Thus, the extreme model, properly employed, may actually be used in a sense almost directly opposed to that for which it was created. In each of the more useful versions of the production-possibility model, an "excess burden" is present, at least for some individuals or groups, if we define "excess burden" as the existence of a negative production-possibility or income effect. In important and relevant situations, the excess burdens are paralleled by excess benefits so that no general welfare conclusions may be attained.

The two analytical models will be reviewed briefly in Section I. In Section II, the position of government in these models will be carefully examined. The case most favorable to the production-possibility approach will be discussed in Section III. Here the implications of the restricting assumptions will be analyzed. Section IV will develop a more useful, although less concise, approach.

7. By this I shall mean the generalized argument which demonstrates, by the use of the standard indifference-opportunity curves for the single individual, the presence of an excess burden of a particular consumption excise tax over an income tax of equal amount imposed on the individual.

Much of this analysis has been suggested but not fully developed in the critical papers cited,[8] and my conclusions are roughly identical with those of the recent contributors.[9] Finally, I shall try to extend the particular contribution of this paper to some of the broader methodological issues which are suggested.

I

The Barone analysis directly suggests that the imposition of a tax, whether it is levied on the consumption of a particular commodity or upon income, reduces the range of opportunities open to the individual. In terms of the standard diagrams, the opportunity curve is shifted and/or rotated toward the origin. This implied tax-induced reduction in real income is one feature of the argument to which objection has been raised. The question is asked: How can the mere imposition of a tax change the opportunities open to the community? The tax in itself does nothing toward modifying either the quantity of real resources available or the range of techniques with which it is possible to employ these resources. The alternative construction is based, therefore, upon the explicit assumption of fixed production possibilities both for the community *and* for the representative individual or consumer whose comparative states of well-being are to be examined. (As will be shown, it is in this shift from the community to the individual that the main difficulties arise.) This production-possibility approach removes any trace of a differential "income" effect from the impact of an excise tax. The excise tax differs from the income tax only as the tax-induced change in relative prices produces a different consumption pattern. The representative individual remains on the same consumption-possibility frontier. The excise tax is more burdensome only in so far as the new equilibrium position is further away from that position in which the necessary marginal conditions for Paretian optimality are fully satisfied. Whether or not a particular excise tax exerts this effect is held

8. The following should be added: George F. Break, "Excise Tax Burdens and Benefits," *American Economic Review,* XLIV (1954), 577-94; Cecil G. Phipps, "Friedman's 'Welfare' Effects," *Journal of Political Economy,* LX (1952), 332-34; Milton Friedman, "A Reply," *Journal of Political Economy,* LX (1952), 334-36.

9. Especially by Break, *loc. cit.*

to depend strictly on the characteristics of the pre-tax state. In some situations the consumption tax involves a greater burden when compared with the income tax, in others a lesser burden; there is no general conclusion which can be reached *a priori*.

It is with the above criticism of the Barone analysis and the attempted reconstruction aimed to overcome the alleged defect that this paper is concerned. There have also been important objections raised to the "excess burden" analysis on quite different grounds, notably by Little. He attempts to show that, even if all of the Paretian conditions are fully satisfied in the pre-tax state, no differential burden can be proved since the income tax will also act to distort the choice between leisure and other goods. And such distortions may offset those caused by the excise tax. While this criticism is valid for an analysis which compares an excise tax with a real-world income tax, both the Barone analysis and the production-possibility reconstruction shall be considered here as comparing the effects of an excise tax and an income tax which exerts no influence on individual behavior. We shall assume a tax which is completely neutral, even though such a tax is not likely to be found in the real world. In conceptual terms, this tax may best be considered as some sort of lump-sum tax, not an income tax at all.[10] I shall continue to use the term "income" tax, although the required qualifications should be kept in mind.

In the development of the alternative construction, the analyses of Rolph and Break and of Friedman explicitly make use of the assumption of a community of identical individuals.[11] Little does not explicitly state this as a condition of his analysis, but it may be considered implicit in his reasoning.[12] If this simplifying assumption is accepted, the taxing of any single commodity or service in such a community is, in effect, one means of taxing incomes generally.[13] In such a framework the conception of a partial

10. M. J. Bailey has recognized this and specifically refers to an excise tax-lump sum tax comparison rather than the usual, but looser reference to "income" tax. See M. J. Bailey, "The Interpretation and Application of the Compensation Principle," *Economic Journal,* LXIV (1954), 39-52.

11. Rolph and Break, *op. cit.,* p. 49; Friedman, "The 'Welfare' Aspects of an Income Tax and an Excise Tax," *op. cit.,* p. 107; "A Reply," *op. cit.,* p. 335.

12. Little, *op. cit.,* p. 578.

13. The recognition of this point seems to have been the basis of the early arguments of both Gobbi and Pantaleoni to the effect that there is no difference

excise tax has little meaning since any partial tax takes on most of the important characteristics of a general tax.[14] This aspect of the problem will be discussed in Section IV. The analysis of Sections II and III will be based on an acceptance of the world-of-equals postulate.

II

Given a community composed of individuals identical in every respect, are the objections which have been made to the Barone-type analysis fully legitimate? The first point to be noted is that if we are to discuss tax problems, government as an economic unit must also be considered. It is necessary to specify quite clearly the economic characteristics of the governmental entity and also the nature of the fiscal transaction. These essential steps appear often to have been overlooked. Is the tax to be examined imposed initially on a no-tax situation, or may we assume the previous existence of government as a fiscal agency? Obviously the assumption of no prior government is unduly restrictive for general analysis, but it will be useful to accept this assumption at the outset. The next question becomes that concerning the disposition of the tax proceeds. We may assume that the government uses such proceeds to purchase real goods and services or that it returns the revenues directly to individuals as subsidies. We shall find that each of these cases yields a different result.

We shall first consider the case in which government purchases real goods. We assume that individuals are identical in all respects and that no other fiscal operations are carried out. To further simplify the analysis, we may approach the problem by considering a non-monetary economy with two goods. The government is presumed to demand m units of commodity A and n units of com-

in the burden of the two taxes so long as equal amounts are subtracted from the income of the individual. Gobbi, especially, in his strong opposition to the use of the Marshallian consumer's surplus device in this sort of analysis, appears to have sensed vaguely the fundamental error likely to arise from an indiscriminate application of the "excess burden" analysis to real tax issues. See U. Gobbi, "Un preteso difetto delle imposte sui consumi," *Giornale degli economisti,* (1904), I, 296-306; M. Pantaleoni, "L'identità della pressione teorica di qualunque imposta a parità di ammontare e la sua semioteca," *Giornale degli economisti* (1910), I, 293-324.

14. I am indebted to R. A. Musgrave for emphasizing this point in connection with a different, but related, problem.

modity B. It is to collect its tax directly in kind, and the goods so collected are to be used in such a way that the individual's behavior is not affected, for example, to provide foreign aid.

The analysis may be illustrated in the accompanying figure. The curve, A_1B_1, depicts the individual's production (consumption) possibility frontier prior to the tax. His initial position is assumed to be located at *P*. The curve, A_2B_2, depicts the individual's private consumption possibility curve after the tax is collected. It should be noted that for each point on A_1B_1, say P, there corresponds a single point on A_2B_2, such as P′. If the pre-tax state is P and the government demands and collects *m* of A and *n* of B, the individual must move to P′.

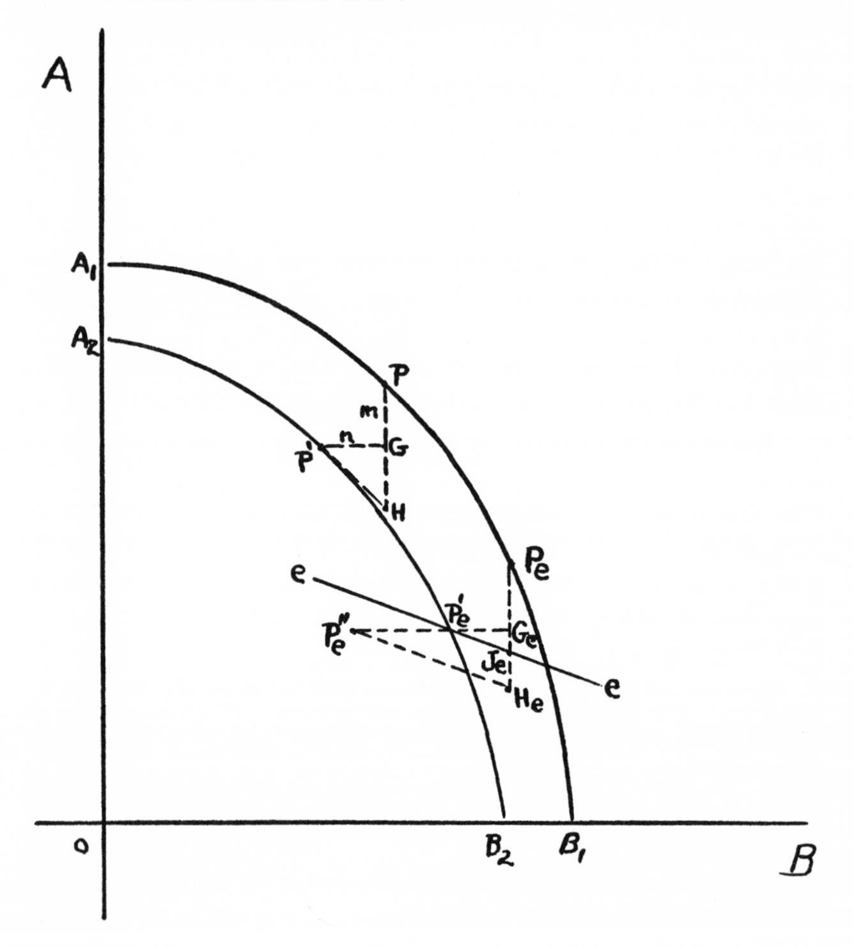

Now it is assumed that the commodity A is made the monetary commodity and that the government collects its taxes in A units, but still desires only *m* of A and *n* of B for collective use. This is the income tax with which we are concerned, and it replaces the tax-in-kind. Figure 1 indicates that the amount of commodity A necessary under these conditions is PH, with the government retaining PG and using the amount GH to trade in the market for commodity B. It will receive precisely the *n* units (P′G) which it needs. Note that, by assuming this income tax to exert no influence on behavior, we are, in effect, stating that the consumption-possibility curve is tangent to an indifference curve at P′.

Now instead of levying the required tax in this non-discriminatory manner we shall assume that the government replaces the income tax with an excise tax. This tax is levied on the consumption of commodity A only. The effect of this tax will be that of changing the rate at which the individual can substitute one commodity for the other in consumption. This change in the price ratio of the two commodities will cause the individual to change his initial production position away from P. He will shift his production toward B and away from A. As he does so, the cost price of B will increase relative to A. But if we make the standard assumptions concerning his indifference curves, his final position must involve an increased relative price of A, the good upon which the excise tax is levied. In other words, the increase in the relative cost price of B as more B is produced cannot be expected fully to offset the decrease in the post-tax relative price of B induced by the tax. The individual must reach a new position of equilibrium such as that shown at P'_e with the corresponding production position shown at P_e. The post-tax relative price ratio is shown as *ee*.

Our purpose is that of comparing the yields of the two taxes. We showed above that the yield of the income tax required to allow a government purchase of *m* of A and *n* of B was PH. We can now show that the yield of the excise tax required to facilitate the same government purchase is P_eJ_e. This is less than PH, and, therefore, we may conclude that the yield of the excise tax is less than the yield of the income tax. This conclusion may be demonstrated by the fact that PG is equal by definition to P_eG_e and similarly P′G is equal to P'_eG_e. Therefore, since the slope of *ee* is less than the slope of the line drawn through P′ and H, the distance P_eJ_e must be less than PH. Fewer dollars of excise tax revenue are needed in order to purchase the same quantity of government goods and services.

Where does this conclusion fit into the comparative tax analysis which we are considering? The traditional analysis has normally started from the premise that the two taxes to be compared provide equal yields. As the above analysis shows, however, two taxes of equal monetary yield cannot produce an unchanged total of real goods and services for government. If we now modify the analysis to fit the standard comparison, we can see that the excise tax which collects an equal money total with the income tax produces a greater amount of public or collective goods and services. If the government collects the amount PH through the income tax it secures only the *m* units of A and *n* units of B. Now assume that it plans to collect the same total through the excise tax. P_eH_e is drawn equal to PH. By collecting P_eH_e the government could retain P_eG_e of A and trade G_eH_e for G_e $P'_e{}'$ of B. The consumption position $P'_e{}'$ lies inside the previously drawn consumption possibility frontier.[15] With the equal monetary yield included as a premise of the analysis, the excise tax imposition will allow a wholly new consumption possibility frontier to be constructed which lies wholly inside the consumption possibility frontier under the income tax of equal yield. We conclude, therefore, that in this extremely simplified two-good world, the excise tax which yields an equal monetary sum with the income tax will reduce private consumption possibilities by a greater amount than the income tax. There is a differential or excess burden of the excise tax over and above that created merely by the distortion of the consumer purchase pattern. We have not introduced the latter effect at any place in the discussion although it may readily be incorporated into the analysis of the figure.

15. The heavier excise tax would, of course, shift the production point away from P_e, and thus the new consumption position $P'_e{}'$. Since identical conclusions are obtained, this shift has not been introduced in the figure above.

The results of this analysis may be generalized to the many-commodity world without difficulty. The results presented above hold so long as the government does not differentially tax those goods which it plans to purchase.[16] If, in our model, the government purchases only commodity A, the commodity which it taxes differentially, then the individual remains on the same consumption-possibility curve with the two taxes which have equal yields in money. It is easy to see that this procedure would be highly unusual, and that we may accept the argument of the model as representing the more typical case.

In the model which we have used above, the taxes were collected in terms of the designated monetary commodity, A. Let us now extend the analysis to apply to a more realistic model which includes many commodities and a separate non-commodity monetary system. We shall retain the identity-of-individuals assumption.

It is first necessary to deflate the actual money yield of the taxes in some way in order to define equality of yield in real terms. This step is necessary in order to eliminate the possibly different effects of the two taxes upon the absolute price level.[17] The procedure involves deflating the money yields by some appropriate price index. Here, as always, the question as to the proper price index arises. Initially, we may specify that the yield of the two taxes be made equivalent in terms of dollars of generalized purchasing power, that is, we assume an index incorporating both final product and factor prices. The absolute price level differences are eliminated, and only the effects of the two taxes on relative prices remain.

Just as in the more simplified model above, the excise tax will cause the price of the taxed good to increase relative to the other goods and services. From this it follows that, unless government purchases goods in precisely the same proportions as the average, in this case, every, consumer (that is, unless government

16. One of the essential contributions of H. P. B. Jenkins has been his emphasis on the necessity of considering government purchases. See H. P. B. Jenkins, "Excise-Tax Shifting and Incidence: A Money-Flows Approach," *Journal of Political Economy,* LXIII (1955), 125-49.

17. Such effects will depend upon the specific monetary framework which is assumed for the analysis.

is also an identical "individual" or some aggregate thereof) a different amount of real goods and services can be purchased with the proceeds of the two taxes providing equal real yield. The change in relative prices will change the "terms of trade" at which government services may be purchased. Except in the exceedingly restrictive case in which the government differentially taxes at higher rates the product which it plans to purchase, more real goods and services can be procured with the proceeds of the excise tax than with those of the income tax of equal real yield.

Thus we reach the same conclusion which we reached in the more highly abstract two-good model. There does exist a differential "income" effect of the excise tax in the normal case.

We may now demonstrate that the same conclusion holds even if we assume that the government returns the proceeds to individuals in full tax-offsetting subsidies provided that any additional fiscal activity of the government takes place. In this situation, even if the tax in question does nothing to shift in any way the consumption-possibility frontier of the individual, the tax-induced change in relative prices will allow the government to purchase a different amount of real goods and services with the proceeds of other taxes in the income tax and the excise tax case.

The results of the analysis may be generalized as follows. If the government purchases real goods and services, either with the tax in question, or with other taxes, the excise tax and the income tax which produce equal yields will result in different private-consumption possibilities for the individual, and, in the normal case, the excise tax will reduce private-consumption possibilities to a greater extent.

III

We may now consider the model in which the production-possibility approach is most appropriate. Three simplifying assumptions are necessary. First, individuals are identical in all respects. Secondly, there are no other fiscal activities undertaken by government. Thirdly, the proceeds of the taxes under consideration are returned to individuals in full tax-offsetting subsidies which exert no supplementary influence on individual behavior. In this model, there can be no "excess burden" or "income" effect as we have defined this term. The government purchases no real goods and services either before or after the new fiscal operation. The total amount of resources available for private disposition is the same before and after the change, and remains unchanged under a switch between the two tax forms.

This model yields the familiar result that if, prior to the action proposed, all of the necessary marginal conditions for Paretian optimality are satisfied, the excise tax will exert a differential burden only because it tends to shift the consumption pattern away from the optimum as represented by individual preferences. From this it appears to follow that, if the initial position is not such that these marginal requirements are met, nothing can be said concerning the relative effects of the two taxes on welfare. There are no "income" effects since the individual remains on the same production-consumption possibility curve. And the substitution effects may improve or worsen individual well-being depending on the conditions prevailing in the pre-tax state.

This conclusion is not fully applicable, and is, in fact, incorrect. In this extreme world-of-equals model, the *initial position must be optimal.* In a world composed of individuals identical both in tastes and in factor endowments and characterized by proportional equivalence between individual and aggregate production functions,[18] *there could be no trade.* Each individual would be a Crusoe, and he would individually adjust his marginal rate of substitution in consumption to that in production. Thus, it is meaningless to speak of competitive or monopoly conditions prevailing in this model. Unless an offsetting excise tax is imposed by government, the imposition of a new excise tax must always involve a greater burden than the equal yield income tax.[19]

18. The rate at which any one individual may substitute one unit of good A for B in production must be equal to the rate at which the economy can substitute n units of A for n of B, n being the number of individuals. This requirement eliminates differential returns to *individual* scales of operation. This suggests, of course, the complete absence of specialization. This extreme requirement is, however, quite necessary if we are to utilize individual production possibility frontiers to represent community production possibility frontiers.

19. We may refer to Friedman's Figure 3, p. 110 (*Essays in Positive Economics*). He states that if the initial position is P_6 rather than P_1, the excise tax would be preferable to the income tax. But an initial position at P_6 is impossible under the assumptions of the model. In a genuine world-of-equals, P_1 remains the only possible position.

The differential burden is not an "excess" burden in the "income" effect sense. The individual remains on the same production-consumption frontier. The burden results solely from the distortion in the individual's consumption pattern, that is, the substitution effect generated by the tax-induced shift in relative prices. It is somewhat singular that this extreme model is the only one in which we may arrive at some reasonably unambiguous conclusions concerning the welfare effects of the two equal yield taxes. Here, since the initial position must be optimal, the income tax is clearly superior to the excise tax. It will make everyone better off and no one worse off than they would be under the comparable excise tax.

The severe limitations of this model may be relaxed but only at the expense of destroying the expositional usefulness. If individuals are assumed to differ either in tastes or in initial factor endowments, trade among individuals takes place, and the individual can, through trade, attain a consumption-possibility frontier which lies wholly outside his private production-possibility frontier. If trade takes place, however, individuals must be classified by market position, and any shift in relative prices will affect different individuals differently. The existence of trade also allows departures from the idealized conditions to be present, and, therefore, no analysis can reach definitive conclusions concerning the relative effects of the two taxes on general welfare. Under certain assumptions about initial conditions, meaningful but hardly useful conclusions can be attained. For example, if individuals are assumed to differ in tastes but to remain identical in factor endowments, the excise tax can be shown to impose a differential burden on all groups, provided that the initial position is Pareto optimal. If the initial position is not "efficient" in this sense, the excise tax can be demonstrated to be more burdensome only if the appropriateness of the compensation principle of the new welfare economics is accepted. If individuals are assumed to differ in factor endowments, no assumptions about the initial position will remove the distributional effects from the analysis.

IV

Any approach toward a more useful analysis must depart from a model less restrictive than that which assumes no other fiscal activities of government, the employment of the revenues in full tax-offsetting subsidies, and the world of identical individuals. In Section II, it was shown that any relaxation of the first two assumptions did involve differential "income" effects of the excise tax. Let us now retain these first two assumptions for the time being and relax only the world-of-equals assumption. This introduces the "partial" tax in the significant sense of the term. We shall assume a many-goods world populated by individuals who differ both in tastes and in factor endowments. We shall assume that the tax is to be levied on a particular group in society which is to be identified by its consumption of a specifically designated commodity. Again it is supposed that the tax can take two possible forms, and that it is supposed to yield the same revenue in either form, this revenue to be defined in units of generalized purchasing power. If the choice is the income tax, this must be levied on those individuals who consume the chosen commodity, and it must be levied not in proportion to income but in proportion to their consumption of the commodity. This cannot be a general income tax, and it is clearly a peculiar sort of fiscal device. It must be related to the consumption of the commodity, but it must not be tied to the consumption in so far as the announcement effects on the individual are concerned. The relevant alternatives for analysis are the partial excise tax and some sort of partial or disproportionate income tax which is to be subtracted directly from the incomes of individuals without modifying the choice patterns on either the demand or the supply side.

The analysis will be clarified if we divide the community into groups, both on the consumption and the production sides of the individual accounts. We separate consumers of the taxed commodity from the non-consumers, and producers of the taxed commodity from the non-producers. It is evident that the consumers of the taxed good, as a group, are made worse off, in their roles as consumers, by the excise tax than by the income tax of equal yield and equal distribution. If, as we are assuming, the proceeds of the tax are returned to taxpayers in full tax-offsetting subsidies, the consumer of the taxed commodity will find his relative position unchanged by the levy of the income tax. But his relative position will be worsened by the equal yield excise tax, even with the full tax-offsetting subsidies. Conversely, the non-consumer will find his relative position improved under the excise tax whereas it would be unchanged under the income tax. The non-consumer pays no tax and receives no subsidy in either case, as a consumer, but in the excise-tax situation he receives a real income boost due to the tax induced reduction in the relative prices of the non-taxed goods and services of the economy.

The analysis is incomplete until we also take into account the effects upon individuals in their roles as producers. The excise tax serves to increase the price of the particular commodity, inclusive of tax, relative to the prices of non-taxed goods and services. This change in relative prices will generate a shift in demand away from the taxed good. The resource adjustments required to meet this shift in demand will decrease the cost or pre-tax price of the taxed good relative to other goods and services, provided only that diminishing returns prevail in the economy. Hence the change in relative prices, exclusive of tax, will cause those individuals owning specialized resources employed in producing the taxed commodity to suffer a real income reduction, while those individuals owning specialized resources employed in producing other goods and services may receive a real income increase.

For any given individual, the net difference in the effects of the two taxes will depend on his position both in the consumption and the factor side of the market for the taxed commodity. If he is a consumer of the taxed good and also a net supplier, there is clearly an "excess burden" of the excise tax. On the other hand, if he is both a non-consumer and a net non-supplier, the excise tax clearly involves a differential benefit for him. In the remaining two cases, the effects on the individual's real income position are indeterminate. If he is a consumer and a non-supplier, he gains as a producer but loses as a consumer. If he is a non-consumer but a net supplier, he gains as a consumer but loses as a producer.

The analysis above has continued to employ the device of the full tax-offsetting subsidies in order to eliminate the difficulties involving government purchases which were discussed in Section II. While this device is useful for purely analytical purposes, its limitations are clear. Since such a fiscal operation would involve neither distributional nor functional significance, meaningful tax comparisons must move beyond this stage.

We may now consider the case in which the government desires to raise a given real sum by taxing the consumers of a particular commodity with the proceeds to be used in granting general subsidies to all individuals in the community. This general subsidy is also defined so as to exert no influence on individual productive behavior. We shall continue to assume that this is the only fiscal operation undertaken by the government.

The range of opportunities open to the consumers of the good selected, either for the excise tax or as the basis for the income tax, will be reduced regardless of the form of the tax. But the levy of the zero-announcement-effect "income" tax on the consumers of the commodity, say A (I shall call this the A-income tax), combined with the corresponding outpayment of the zero-announcement-effect general subsidy, will affect relative prices only as a result of shifts in the demand pattern between the one group and the community at large. The real income of the A-consumers will be reduced; the offsetting subsidies will not be sufficient to keep the members of this group on the same real income level before and after the fiscal operation. On the other hand, the subsidy will increase the real incomes of the non-consumers of A.

How will the imposition of the excise directly on the consumption of commodity A be different? The tax will cause the price of A, inclusive of tax, to increase relative to other prices. This shift in relative prices will be additional to those occasioned by changes in the demand pattern. The tax-induced relative reduction in the average prices of non-A goods and services will allow the non-consumers of A to secure a supplementary real income increase, that is, a real income boost additional to that which would be secured under the A-income tax alternative, provided that these non-consumers are not net producers of A. On the other hand, A-consumers will be subjected to a supplementary real income reduction unless they are also heavy net suppliers of non-A goods and services. It is clear that any particular individual could find his real income reduced or increased by the switch from the income tax to the excise tax and vice versa. But if the consumption of the commodity is relatively concentrated while few highly specialized resources are utilized in its production, the neo-classical emphasis upon individuals in their roles as consumers of the taxed commodity is justified. Such emphasis is faulty, however, if it overlooks the presence of the "excess benefits" as well as the "excess burdens." Both must result from any levy of the excise tax regardless of the initial position.

The conclusions reached above may easily be generalized. Those individuals who consume and produce relatively more of the taxed commodity or service will be subjected to an "excess burden" of the excise tax; those individuals who both consume and produce relatively less of the taxed commodity or service will be subjected to an "excess benefit."

We have continued to employ the assumption that the government engages in no other fiscal activity. When this assumption is relaxed, and the government is allowed to purchase real goods and services, either with the proceeds of the taxes under comparison, or with other revenues, the shift in the private consumption possibilities of the community which was examined in Section II must be introduced. This shift may or may not modify the above conclusions. It is possible that the excise tax, under these conditions, would involve an "excess burden" for all individuals. But it is also possible that some individuals will still receive an "excess benefit."

It may be concluded that the general results of the papers critical of the orthodox excess burden argument are correct. No conclusions can be reached from this sort of analysis relating to the general welfare of the community as a whole. In spite of this, the orthodox analysis does lend itself to consideration of the effects of the partial excise tax somewhat better than its proposed replacement. The production-possibility reconstruction of the comparative tax analysis must be modified. This construction is formally valid only in those extreme situations where the fiscal action can be truly general on both sides of the government budget; that is, in those situations where no individuals or groups are differentially affected. This is essential if the "representative" individual model is to be useful. A large part of the analysis of this paper has been devoted to showing that such situations are difficult to construct, and when constructed, carry with them implications which are unintended by their creators. In the real world, fiscal action must always exert differential effects; tax measures must normally be partial. And, in so far as this is true, there will exist excess burdens of an excise tax as well as excess benefits.

The critical papers have correctly identified the weak spot in the Barone sort of analysis. This lies in its concentration on the single individual or group who cannot be representative. Such a concentration tends to cause the effects imposed upon other non-representative individuals or groups to be overlooked, effects which will normally be in the opposing or offsetting direction. We have demonstrated that the alternative production-possibility approach also has its limitations. By forcing the analysis into such a mold that a single individual can be used to represent the whole community, many facets of the problems which arise because of differential effects upon separate individuals or groups tend to be obscured.

V

Friedman has employed the excise-tax–income-tax comparison to illustrate his approach to economic theory. It will be useful to place the analysis of this paper in the broader and more general methodological setting. The essential issue concerns the meaning and application of partial-equilibrium analysis.

It is clear that Friedman intends partial-equilibrium analysis to be used primarily as a form of general-equilibrium analysis.[20] This approach suggests that the economist, while recognizing the

20. Friedman, "The Marshallian Demand Curve," *Journal of Political Economy,* LVII (1949), 490.

general interdependence among all the variables of his system, simplifies reality to some manageable proportions by constructing a model of the behavior of a representative individual, consumer, or firm. Thus, the behavior of the whole economy is mirrored in the actions of a sub-economy smaller than itself. And, if the representative unit is carefully chosen so as to possess the relevant characteristics of the parent group, positive general equilibrium results may be obtained.

Granted the advantages of this approach for many real problems, there appears to be another type of partial analysis for which the representative-man construction is not appropriate. The problem under consideration may require that the behavior of an atypical subgroup smaller than the total group be analyzed. This sort of analysis must remain partial both in subject and in results. It applies to a group which is not, and cannot be, characteristic of the total group; it cannot, therefore, yield conclusions which are applicable for the whole group.

If we limit analysis to comparative statics, there must be present, even for the second sort of partial analysis, offsetting effects on the behavior of other atypical individuals or groups. But the offsets may be conceptually distributed in any number of ways.[21] In any analysis of the behavior of a particular group, the offsetting changes may be allowed to take place in variables outside the set which influences the behavior of that group. And the neglect of these offsets may not, in some cases, modify the predictive value of the analysis.

The choice between these two approaches to partial equilibrium analysis depends on the problem to be solved. The comparative tax analysis illustrates this point well. If the tax is relatively small and it is to be levied on the consumption of a commodity which is not widely consumed, the Barone analysis seems preferable to the production-possibility analysis in many respects. The user of such an analysis must, however, take full account of the limitations imposed upon him, especially those involving any extension of the analysis to general welfare conclusions. On the

21. Cf. M. J. Bailey, "The Marshallian Demand Curve," *Journal of Political Economy,* LXII (1954), 260.

other hand, if the tax is on a single good which is widely consumed, or is on a wide range of goods, the production of which looms as relatively important in the whole economy, the production-possibility approach seems more appropriate. But again the user must recognize the limitations which his method imposes; in this case, the obscuring of the differential effects which any real world fiscal operation must generate.

The choice here is analogous to that facing the economist who attempts to construct the individual demand curve. For an important, widely consumed, commodity, a Friedman-Bailey type of demand curve which holds individual real income roughly constant, or, in other words, which assumes full offsetting variations in other prices and/or money income within the budget of the single consumer, is clearly the more appropriate analytical tool. But, if the consumption of the commodity is concentrated and uneven, the Hicksian demand curve which neglects the offsetting variations may yield superior results since these variations may well take place largely outside the budget of the individual consumer under consideration.[22] While Giffen's paradox is impossible within the representative-man context, it is possible, although not probable, for the "poorer labouring classes."

22. Friedman appears to agree. See his reply to Bailey, "A Reply," *Journal of Political Economy,* LXII (1954), 261-66.

VIII

FEDERALISM AND FISCAL EQUITY*

FISCAL relations between central and subordinate units of government have become an important problem area in the United States during the last two decades.[1] Increasing attention has been, and is being, given to the more practical policy proposals aimed at accomplishing specific short-run objectives. While this may have been necessary, perhaps too little attention has been placed upon the study and the formulation of the long-run objectives of an inter-governmental fiscal structure.[2] This paper seeks to formulate a specific long-run goal for policy and will discuss the advantages which might be expected to arise from its general acceptance.

I

A distinct group of problems immanently arises when a single political unit possessing financial authority in its own right contains within its geographical limits smaller political units also possessing financial authority.[3] These problems become especially important

*Reprinted without substantial change from *American Economic Review,* XL (September, 1950), 583-99.

1. The most general survey of the whole field published to date is: U.S. Congress, Senate, *Federal, State and Local Government Fiscal Relations,* Sen. Doc. 69, 78th Cong., 1st Sess. (Washington: Government Printing Office, 1943). Other competent works include: J. A. Maxwell, *The Fiscal Impact of Federalism in the United States* (Cambridge: Harvard University Press, 1946); Jane P. Clark, *The Rise of a New Federalism* (New York: Columbia University Press, 1938); G. C. S. Benson, *The New Centralization* (New York: Farrar and Rinehart, 1941).

2. One important work in the field is concerned with this aspect: B. P. Adarkar, *The Principles and Problems of Federal Finance* (London: P. S. King and Sons, 1933).

3. Financial authority may be defined as the power of a governmental unit to collect revenues from contained fiscal resources and to expend such revenues in the performance of governmental functions. *Cf.* Adarkar, *op. cit.,* p. 31.

in a federal polity since the financial authority of the subordinate units is constitutionally independent of that of the central government. In a federalism, two constitutionally independent fiscal systems operate upon the fiscal resources of individual citizens.[4]

The fiscal system of each unit of government is limited in its operation by the geographical boundaries of that unit; it can withdraw resources for the financing of public services only from those available within this area. If the subordinate units are required independently to finance certain traditionally assigned functions, fiscal inequalities among these units will be present unless the fiscal capacities are equivalent. There will be differences in the number and/or the standard of the public services performed for, and/or the burden of taxes levied upon, the owners of economic resources within the separate units. The nature and the extent of these differences, and the difficulties involved in their elimination, constitute the elements of the over-all fiscal problem of the federal polity.

Before World War II (after which the relevant trends may have been somewhat modified), the situation became progressively more acute in the United States. This can be attributed largely to the three following parallel historical trends: First, the continual industrialization, specialization, and integration of the economy on a national scale tended to concentrate high income receivers in specific geographical areas. Second, there was an extension of the range of governmental activity at all levels in the political hierarchy. This required the diversion of greater and greater shares of the total of economic resources through the fiscal mechanism. Third, this extension of governmental activity at the lower levels of government (and in peacetime at the top level) took place largely through the increase in the provision of the social services. This, when coupled with the type of tax structure prevailing, increased the amount of real income redistribution accomplished by the operation of the fiscal system.

4. The individual must deal with three or more fiscal systems, federal, state, and one or more local units. Local financial authority is, however, derivative from that of the state, and for present purposes, the combined state-local fiscal system will be considered as one unit.

In 1789, a significant share of economic activity was limited to local markets; there was relatively little areal specialization of production. Governmental services were performed predominantly by the local units which were drawn up roughly to correspond in area to the extent of the local markets. Rapid developments in transportation and communication led to an ever-increasing specialization of resources. The economy grew more productive, but the inequalities in personal incomes and wealth increased. This emerging inequality was both inter-personal and inter-regional; expanding individual differences were accompanied by closer concentration of the higher income recipients in the more favored areas. This created disparities among the states in their capacities to support public services.

These fiscal divergencies were not conspicuous, however, until the extension of governmental activity caused the traditional sources of revenue to become inadequate. As greater amounts of revenue were required at all levels, conflicts over revenue sources among state units, and between states and the central government, arose.

The form which the extension of governmental activity took was an important determining factor in making the problem more difficult. Even with the increasing costs of government, inter-regional disparities in fiscal capacity would not have been accentuated had not the extension taken place largely through the expanded provision of the social services. Had the role of government remained "protective," and thus the fiscal system conformed more closely to the benefit or *quid pro quo* principle, richer units would have needed greater governmental expenditures. Only when the "social" state appeared did the divergency between need and capacity become clear. As more government services were provided equally to all citizens, or upon some basis of personal need, the discrepancies between the capacities and needs of the subordinate units arose.

The emerging fiscal problem has been only one of many created by the progressive national integration of the economic system within a decentralized political structure. This development has caused many students to view the political structure as outmoded and the federal spirit as a thing of the past.[5] The federal polity, in this view, has outlived its usefulness, and the conditions which made it necessary as a stage in the process of political development no longer prevail.[6] It is true that complete political centralization would resolve the peculiar fiscal problem of federalism. If there were only one fiscal system, as there would be in a unitary form of government, regional differences in standards of public services and/or burdens of taxation would not exist.[7] But political centralization as a proposal for solution is precluded if we accept the desirability of maintaining the federal form. The approach taken in this paper accepts the federal political structure, with the existence of the states as constitutionally independent units sovereign within specified areas. Thus, the problem is reduced to that of formulating a solution within this given framework.

The same problem of fiscal inequality is, of course, present among local units of government within the same state unit. However, the scope for adjustment by non-fiscal means, through political or administrative devices (local government consolidation, state assumption of local functions, etc.), seems broader in state-local relations. The policy proposals stemming from the analysis which follows presume a fixed political structure. But it should be emphasized that both the analysis and the policy implications can be extended to inter-local unit fiscal adjustment as well as to interstate fiscal adjustment. Subsequent discussion will, however, be limited to the latter.

II

The ideal type adjustment can be presented in reference to the relative fiscal systems of different state units which possess the same fiscal capacity. If all states were approximately identical in per capita incomes and wealth, the burden of taxation upon resources would not necessarily be equal in all. Neither would

5. See Roy F. Nichols, "Federalism vs. Democracy," *Federalism as a Democratic Process* (New Brunswick: Rutgers University Press, 1942), p. 50.

6. Gordon Greenwood, *The Future of Australian Federalism* (Melbourne: Melbourne University Press, 1946), p. viii.

7. The proposal for integration and unification of the fiscal systems at different levels has been excellently presented by S. E. Leland. See, for example, his "The Relations of Federal, State, and Local Finance," *Proceedings, National Tax Association,* XXIII (1930), 94-106.

the general level nor the distribution of public services be equivalent. Some states might choose to tax more heavily and thus provide a higher level of public services than other units equal in fiscal potential. The criterion of comparison must be some balance between the two sides. Both the level of tax burden and the range of publicly provided services must be included. Units of equal fiscal capacity should be able to provide equivalent services at equivalent tax burdens.

An intergovernmental transfer system can be worked out which would allow state units originally unequal in fiscal capacity to provide equal services at equal rates of taxation. The explicit objective of such a system would be the placing of all state units in a position which would allow them to provide a national average level of public services at average tax rates.[8] Immediately there arises the difficult task of determining average rates of taxation and average standards of public service. A more important objection to the statement of the policy goal in this form is that it appears in terms of adjustment among organic state units. Equality in terms of states is difficult to comprehend,[9] and it carries with it little ethical force for its policy implementation. And, is there any ethical precept which implies that states should be placed in positions of equal fiscal ability through a system of intergovernmental transfers?

If the interstate differences in fiscal capacity can be traced through to their ultimate impact upon individuals, and a policy objective formulated in inter-personal terms, it would seem that greater support could be marshalled for interstate fiscal equalization. Any discussion of the operations of a fiscal system or systems upon different individuals or families must be centered around some concept of fiscal justice. And although fiscal justice in its all-inclusive sense is illusory and almost purely relative to the particular social environment considered, there has been contained in all formulations the central tenet of equity in the sense of "equal

8. This is the policy objective of the National Adjustment Grants proposed by the Royal Commission on Dominion-Provincial Relations after a study of the problem in Canada. See *Report of the Royal Commission on Dominion-Provincial Relations,* Book II, *Recommendations* (1940).

9. See R. McQueen, "Economic Aspects of Federalism: A Prairie View," *Canadian Journal of Economics and Political Science,* I (1935), 353.

treatment for equals" or equal treatment for persons dissimilar in no relevant respect.[10] This basic principle has been so widely recognized that it has not been expressly stated at all times, but rather implicitly assumed. Whether or not this principle is consistent with maximizing "social utility,"[11] it is essential as a guide to the operations of a liberal democratic state, stemming from the same base as the principle of the equality of individuals before the law.[12]

The statement of "equal treatment for equals" as a central principle immediately raises the question of defining precisely the conditions of equality which are relevant in fiscal policy, and more especially intergovernmental fiscal policy. Traditionally, rather objective measures or standards have been accepted, and the divergency between the quality represented in these and subjective or psychic equality has been neglected. Money income and estimated property values in money have therefore been used as the bases for judging individual standing for tax purposes. Some allowance has been made for family size, for income source, and for other differences generating real income effects, but differences in geographical location have not been held to warrant differences in tax treatment.[13] There seems no special reason why intergovernmental fiscal adjustment policy should be set apart in this regard from national government tax policy. Thus, "equals" in the following analysis are individuals equal in those objective economic circumstances traditionally employed in the calculation of

10. "Different persons should be treated similarly unless they are dissimilar in some relevant respect." (A. C. Pigou, *A Study in Public Finance* [London: Macmillan, 1929], p. 9.)

11. If all aspects of equality, including utility or pleasure creation, are included in the definition of "equals," then the principle will be directed toward maximum "social utility" but will be useless due to the impossibility of application. This would be true because any application would require some interpersonal comparison of utility. Any realistic definition of "equals" must omit subjective attributes of equality; therefore, the application of the principle does not necessarily maximize "social utility."

12. *Cf.* J. S. Mill, *Principles of Political Economy* (Boston: Charles C. Little and James Brown, 1848), II, 352.

13. Differences in geographical location perhaps cause significant differences in real incomes among particular individuals, but these would seem to be offsetting when large numbers of individuals are considered. If the real incomes of all, or large numbers of, individuals, were increased or decreased by location in particular geographical areas, then these differences would become relevant for fiscal policy.

national government tax burdens.[14] Through the use of this definition of equals and the adoption of the equity principle, a formal solution to the fiscal problem of federalism can be worked out. This allows the problem to be isolated and separated from the much more difficult one of the distribution of fiscal burdens and benefits among unequals, in which an explicit formulation of "justice" is impossible.

III

What is equal fiscal treatment for equals? The orthodox answer has been almost wholly in reference to the tax side alone, the implication being that if tax burdens of similarly situated individuals were identical, the equity criterion would be satisfied. The necessity of including the benefit side of the fiscal account has been overlooked completely in many cases, and understressed in all.[15] The object of comparison should be the aggregate fiscal pressure upon the individual or family, not tax treatment alone. The balance between the contributions made and the value of public services returned to the individual should be the relevant figure. This "fiscal residuum" can be negative or positive. The fiscal structure is equitable in this primary sense only if the fiscal residua of similarly situated individuals are equivalent.

It is next necessary to define the appropriate political structure to be considered in its relative impact on individuals. In a federal polity, the individual has a plurality of political units with which to deal fiscally. Two or more independent fiscal systems act upon his economic resources, subtract from those resources through compulsory taxation, and provide in return certain public services. In this situation, what becomes of the criterion of equity postulated? Each political unit may treat equals equally.[16] If this

14. This analysis does not require any particular set of attributes of equality. All that is required is that geographical location not be included.

15. For a further elaboration on this and related points, see "The Pure Theory of Government Finance: A Suggested Approach," *supra,* Essay I.

16. This requirement has been expressly stated by one student of the problem. "In a democratic society considerations of equity demand that governmental programs *at each level* treat all citizens in similar circumstances uniformly" (italics supplied). (Byron L. Johnson, *The Principle of Equalization Applied to the Allocation of Grants in Aid,* Bureau of Research and Statistics Memo. No. 66 [Washington: Social Security Administration, 1947], p. 88.)

were done, individuals similarly situated would be subjected to equal fiscal treatment only if they were citizens of the same subordinate unit of government. There would be no guarantee that equals living in different subordinate units would be equally treated at all. Therefore, the principle of equity must be extended to something other than individual governmental units to be of use in solving the fiscal problem of federalism.

The limitation of the application of the equity principle to single fiscal systems within a federal polity can be questioned. It can be plausibly established that the appropriate unit should be the combined fisc, including all the units in the political hierarchy. The argument can take either or both of two forms.

1. In the United States, the economy, for all practical purposes, is national in scope. In large part, resources are allocated in response to incentives provided in a nation-wide market for both final products and for productive services. Goods are sold and equities are traded nationally. The fiscal system represents the political unit in its direct impact upon the economy. Therefore, since the economy is national, the matching political structure must be considered as one unit in its operations upon that economy.[17] If it be accepted that one of the guiding principles in the operation of a fiscal system should be that of "least price distortion,"[18] or least interference with "efficient" resource allocation consistent with the attainment of other specific objectives, the necessity of this approach becomes clear. The principle of equal treatment of equals is consistent with that of least price distortion only if the "treatment" refers to that imposed by a political unit coincident in area with the economic entity. This is, in the United States, the whole political structure, central and local. For, in a federal structure with economically heterogeneous subordinate units, some interference with the proper resource allocation necessarily arises, unless some inter-area fiscal transfers are made.

17. Accepting this does not imply that the political structure should be one unit as has been proposed. There may be, and in my opinion are, definite values to be gained in maintaining a decentralized political structure. The purpose of this paper is that of showing how this decentralization might be retained while still solving the fiscal problem.

18. F. C. Benham, "What is the Best Tax System?" *Economica*, IX (1942), 116.

Fiscal pressures are economic in nature, whether expressed as net burdens or net benefits. If states are not identical in fiscal capacity, the people in the low capacity (low income) states must be subjected to greater fiscal pressure (higher taxation and/or lower value of public services) than people in high capacity states. If "equals" are thus pressed more in one area than in another, there will be provided an incentive for migration of both human and non-human resources into the areas of least fiscal pressures. Resources respond to market-determined economic reward, plus fiscal balance. If the fiscal balance for equals is not made equivalent for all areas of the economy, a considerable distortion of resources from the allocation arising as a result of economic criteria alone might result. The whole fiscal structure should be as neutral as is possible in a geographic sense.[19] An individual should have the assurance that wherever he should wish to live in the nation, the over-all fiscal treatment which he receives will be approximately the same.

It seems somewhat anomalous that states are forced through constitutional provision to remain parts of a national economy in the market sense and yet are forced to act as if they were completely independent economic units in their fiscal operations. This was recognized by William H. Jones in 1887, when he proposed a system of centrally collected taxes shared equally per head among states.[20] Requiring state areas to remain integrated in the national economy is inconsistent with the forcing of the governmental units of these areas to act as if the economies were fiscally separate and independent. This inconsistency can only be removed by

19. This should not be taken to imply that complete neutrality in this sense could ever be reached. Even with a transfer system worked out along the proposed lines, differences among states would always be present to provide some distortionary effects. In the non-geographic sense, the fiscal structure will, and should, have some distortionary effects, if the whole system is redistributive.

20. ". . . so long as we persist in applying the principle of autonomous State taxation under Federal forms, and Federal principles of trade and intercourse for purposes of Federal autonomy, the malady will stick to the patient.

"This mingling of autonomous State taxes and Federal principles of free interstate trade and citizenship for purposes of Federal autonomy, is contrary to both the letter and spirit of the Federal Constitution." (William H. Jones, *Federal Taxes and State Expenses* [New York: G. P. Putnam's Sons, 1887], pp. 86-87.)

centralization of fiscal authority or by the provision of some intergovernmental fiscal adjustment.

2. The appropriateness of using the whole political structure as the unit in fiscal equity considerations can be justified in another way. Prior to the impact of the fiscal system, the income distribution arises largely as a result of the payment for resources in accordance with productivity criteria and competitive conditions established on a national basis. The fiscal system is the major means through which this income distribution is redressed toward one which is more ethically acceptable. It follows, then, that the fiscal system, in carrying out this function, should operate in a general manner over the whole area of the economy determining the original distribution. The generality with which the fisc can be operated has been held to be one of its important advantages over redistribution methods which entail particularistic or discriminatory interference with the economic mechanism. But unless the fiscal system is considered that of the whole hierarchy this advantage of generality is lost, and the system necessarily operates in a geographically discriminatory fashion.

The application of the equity principle on the basis of considering the whole political hierarchy as the appropriate unit will yield substantially different results from its application on the basis of considering separate governmental units in isolation. If there are subordinate units of varying economic characteristics within the central government area, the equity principle applied to the whole hierarchy will require that the central government take some action to transfer funds from one area to another. Thus, the central government, considered alone, must violate the orthodox equity precept since it must favor the equals residing in the low capacity units. The central financial authority must enter the process and treat equals unequally in order to offset the divergencies in the income and wealth levels of the subordinate units.[21]

The necessity of assigning this rôle to the central unit in no way implies that the over-all fiscal system be unified in the

21. "The position that the federal government would occupy in the scheme is that of filling in the gaps of unevenness as between one state and another." (Adarkar, *op. cit.*, p. 195.)

sense that all financial decisions be made by one authority. Subordinate units should be able to retain complete authority. Neither the tax burdens nor the standards of public service need be equal for "equals" in any of the states. Satisfaction of the equity criterion requires only that the residua be substantially the same.

The policy objective for intergovernmental transfers then becomes one, reduced to individual terms, of providing or ensuring "equal fiscal treatment for equals." If this objective is attained the individual's place of residence will no longer have a significant effect upon his fiscal position. Persons earning the same income and possessing the same amount of property will no longer be subjected to a much greater fiscal pressure in Mississippi than in New York, solely because of residence in Mississippi.

That a much greater and more effective force can be mustered in support of a transfer system worked out on this basis does not seem open to question. Reduced in this way to a problem of fiscal equity among individuals, the need for inter-area transfers becomes meaningful. Although the results of the working out of such a proposed system would perhaps differ little, if at all, from those forthcoming from a system based upon equalizing the fiscal capacities of the state units, the former carries with it considerable ethical force for its implementation while the latter does not. The ideal of "equal treatment for equals" is superior to that of equalization among organic state units.

IV

The following arithmetical illustration is presented to show how the use of the equity principle can lead to a determinate system of transfers in a simplified model. Assume that in a hypothetical federal government, X, there are two states, A and B. The total population of X is six citizens, with three residing in each state. Their names are A-1, A-2, A-3, B-1, B-2, B-3. The economic characteristics of X are such that in A, two skilled workers and one unskilled worker can be employed, while in B, one skilled worker and two unskilled workers can be employed. Differences in the natural abilities of the six men are such that only three are equipped to do the skilled work, A-1, A-2, and B-1.

The other three must do unskilled work. There are no non-pecuniary advantages to employment in either state. The six men are substantially similar in all other respects. The relative money incomes for the two groups are $10,000 per year for the skilled workers, and $1,000 per year for the unskilled. Therefore, A has two citizens receiving $10,000 and one receiving $1,000, while B has one $10,000 man and two $1,000 men.

Let it be assumed further that the central government imposes a progressive income tax amounting to 10 per cent of the higher incomes and 5 per cent of the lower incomes. All of its revenue is derived from this source. States A and B impose proportional taxes at the rate of 10 per cent on incomes. All their revenue is derived from this source. The tax liability of each of the citizens then is as follows:

NAME	COLLECTED BY X	COLLECTED BY A OR B	TOTAL
A-1	$1,000	$1,000	$2,000
A-2	1,000	1,000	2,000
A-3	50	100	150
B-1	1,000	1,000	2,000
B-2	50	100	150
B-3	50	100	150

It can be easily seen that if tax liability alone is considered, the over-all fiscal structure is equitable in the primary sense. Equals are treated equally. But if both sides of the fiscal account are included, glaring inequities in the treatment of equals appear.

Now, let it be assumed that both the central government, X, and states A and B, expend funds in such a manner that all citizens within their respective jurisdictions benefit equally from publicly provided services. The central government collects a total of $3,150 and when expended each citizen gets a value benefit of $525 from services provided by that unit. State A collects $2,100 from its three citizens, and each gets in return a value benefit of $700 from public services provided by A. State B collects $1,200 and each citizen thus receives only $400 in value benefit from public services provided by B. The final fiscal position of each of the citizens is represented in the following:

NAME	TOTAL TAXES	TOTAL BENEFITS	FISCAL RESIDUUM
A-1	$2,000	$1,225	$ 775
A-2	2,000	1,225	775
A-3	150	1,225	–1,075
B-1	2,000	925	1,075
B-2	150	925	– 775
B-3	150	925	– 775

B-1 is taxed at equal rates with his equals, A-1 and A-2, by both the central government and the state, and receives the same benefits from the central unit, but he receives $300 less in benefits from his state. His fiscal residuum is $1,075 (taxes over benefits) as compared with $775 for his equals. Likewise, the fiscal residuum of B-2 and B-3 is a negative $775 (benefits over taxes) while that of their equal, A-3, is a negative $1,075.

If a transfer of $200 were made among the set of high income equals in this model, from State A to State B, thus reducing the residuum or net tax of B-1 by $200 and increasing that of A-1 and A-2 by $100 each, then each of this group would end up with a residuum of $875. A further transfer of $200 from A-3 to B-2 and B-3 would equalize the negative residua of the low income equals at $875. Thus, a total transfer of $400 from A to B would enable the equals to be placed in identical fiscal positions.

This model presents the use of the equity principle in its most favorable abstraction. Certain major qualifications must be made if the principle is to be universally applicable even in such structurally simple models. In the above model, both state units imposed taxes at the same flat proportional rate and distributed benefits equally per head, while the central government imposed progressive tax rates and distributed benefits equally among its citizens. It is necessary to examine these conditions and trace through the effects of possible changes upon the results. First of all, it can be shown that the central government acting alone can vary the progressiveness or redistributiveness of its fiscal system (either on the tax or expenditure side, or both) without in any way affecting the resulting transfer total.[22] This is, of course, due to the fact that the central government system, in principle at least, treats equals equally, and thus no action carried out by this system alone would affect the existing inequalities among equals.

Second, it can be shown that the transfer total is not changed by a simple increase (decrease) in the desires of the citizens of one state for public services. The result will be changed only if, in the process of providing the increased (decreased) services, the redistributiveness of the state fiscal system is affected. For example, either of the states in the above model, desiring to provide additional services, could levy equal per head poll taxes of any amount without changing the required transfer total at all.

This is not the case, however, when the amount of redistribution carried out in the operation of either or both of the state fiscal systems is changed. Such a change can be carried out by shifts in the allocation of tax burdens or benefits among the different income classes, or through altering the total amounts of economic resources entering the fiscal systems. The limiting case is that in which neither state system is at all redistributive, both operating on purely benefit principles.[23] In this case, each individual receives in value-benefits the equivalence of contributions made, i.e., has a zero residuum. Thus, whatever the income differences among the units, equals are equally treated, and no required transfer is indicated. Thus, it can be stated that as the

22. This can be illustrated by changing the above model to one in which the central government collects all its tax revenues from the three high income receivers. The resulting individual fiscal positions are then as follows:

Name	Total Tax	Total Benefit	Residuum
A-1	$2,050	$1,225	$ 825
A-2	2,050	1,225	825
A-3	100	1,225	—1,125
B-1	2,050	925	1,125
B-2	100	925	−825
B-3	100	925	−825

It can be seen that a transfer of $400 will again place equals in identical fiscal positions. Absolute differences among equals have not been changed by the increase in the progression of the central government tax structure. It will be noted, however, that the fiscal positions of the citizens of B have been improved relative to those of A's citizens.

23. A special form of this limiting case is that in which neither state levies taxes or provides public services.

fiscal system of either of the state units is shifted more toward operation on a benefit basis, i.e., is made less redistributive, the required transfer between the high income state and the low income state is reduced. Conversely, as either system is made more redistributive, a greater transfer is necessary to satisfy the equity criterion.[24] This dependence of the resulting transfer total upon the redistributiveness of the state fiscal systems creates difficult problems in the use of the principle as a direct guide for policy. Since a state unit can by its own action in shifting its internal fiscal structure affect the amount of funds transferred to or away from that state, the practical working out of the transfer system would make necessary some determination of a standard state fiscal structure as the basis for calculation.[25] It is also noted that the transfers are among equals; bloc transfers among states will satisfy the equity criterion only if made in a specific fashion. These and many other more technical problems make a precise application of the equity principle in the real world extremely difficult, but should not serve to prevent its use as a proximate standard for intergovernmental fiscal policy.

A specific type or method of intergovernmental fiscal adjustment is suggested from the above analysis. This is geographically discriminatory central government personal income taxation. Central government income tax rates could be made to vary from state

24. These effects can easily be seen by imposing changed conditions in the original model. Assume now that State A, instead of levying proportional tax rates, adopts a progressive income tax which increases the tax burden on its high income citizens, A-1 and A-2, to $1,050 each, and reduces the tax burden on A-3 to zero. Assume that the distribution of the benefits in both states and B's tax rates remain the same as before. The fiscal positions then are as follows:

Name	Total Taxes	Total Benefits	Fiscal Residuum
A-1	$2,050	$1,225	$ 825
A-2	2,050	1,225	825
A-3	50	1,225	−1,175
B-1	2,000	925	1,075
B-2	150	925	−775
B-3	150	925	−775

In this model, a transfer of $166.67 among the three high income individuals, and $266.67 among the low income individuals is required, or a total of $433.34, as compared to the total of $400 before the change in A's tax structure was made.

25. Applied to the existing structure in the United States this would not present serious difficulties since various state fiscal structures are substantially similar both on the tax and the expenditure side.

to state so as to offset differences in state fiscal capacities.[26] This method of adjustment, by varying personal income tax rates among equals, could come closest to achieving the equity goal. In effect, it would limit the transfers to those among "equals." In the first model above, central government taxes on A-1 and A-2 would be increased from $1,000 to $1,100, while those on B-1 would be reduced from $1,000 to $800. Central government income taxes on A-3 would be increased from $50 to $250, while those on B-2 and B-3 would be reduced from $50 to a negative tax of $50.

Adjustment through the central governmental personal income tax system has another major advantage in that it allows the necessary inter-area transfer of funds to take place without any necessary increase in the total amount of federal revenue. This is an important feature in this era of big central government. Any other transfer method, either in the form of grants to states or geographically discriminatory central government expenditure, requires, initially at least, that a greater share of economic resources be diverted to flow through the central government fiscal mechanism. A further advantage of this adjustment system is that it does not conflict with either the revered principle of financial responsibility or that of state fiscal independence, both of which are so often encountered in discussions of grant-in-aid policy.[27]

Geographically discriminatory personal income taxation by the central government probably would, however, have to hurdle a very significant constitutional barrier before coming into existence in the United States. The courts have held repeatedly that the constitutional uniformity of taxation required was geographical in nature.[28] Although accomplishing the same purpose as a system of positive revenue transfers, this method would appear more violative of traditional, though erroneous, equity precepts.[29] A

26. Adarkar included both geographically discriminatory central government taxation and geographically discriminatory central government expenditure as appropriate adjusting devices. (*Op. cit.*, p. 195.)

27. See the following section.

28. See *Head Money Cases,* 112 US 580; *Knowlton v. Moore,* 178 US 41; *Flint v. Stone Tracy Co.,* 220 US 107.

29. The apparent anomaly here can be attributed in large part to the doctrinal errors made in economic and fiscal theory which have caused the expenditure side to be treated as a less important area of study than the tax side. Differing rates of federal taxation in different states would probably be declared uncon-

more practical objection to this method is that individuals probably respond more quickly to tax burden differentials (especially direct taxes) than to differentials in public service standards. Therefore, if income tax rates vary from state to state in some direct correlation with per capita incomes, even though the system of rates were calculated so as to provide exact equality (to equals) in all states in over-all fiscal treatment, there might still be distortionary resource allocative effects due to this "tax illusion."

Any method of adjustment which involves the federal collection of revenue and subsequent transfer to state governmental units via specific or bloc grants is inferior to the tax adjustment method in so far as the equity criterion alone is considered. A system of grants based upon the equity principle could do little more than utilize the Canadian proposals. States could be placed in a position to treat citizens in the same manner fiscal-wise as their equals in all other states. But states would not necessarily, or probably, choose to do so. Differences in the allocation of both burdens and benefits would be present. Nevertheless, the resultant inequities in the treatment of "equals" would be due to state political decisions, not to the fact that citizens were resident of the state per se. The differences in the treatment of equals could be reduced to insignificance in comparison to those now present.

V

The mere acceptance of the equity principle in discussions concerning the fiscal problem of federalism can yield important results. First of all, upon its acceptance inter-area transfers do not represent outright subsidization of the poorer areas, do not represent charitable contributions from the rich to the poor, and are not analogous to the concept of ability to pay in the interpersonal sense. The principle establishes a firm basis for the claim that the citizens of the low income states within a national economy possess the "right" that their states receive sums sufficient to enable these citizens to be placed in positions of fiscal equality with their equals in other states. A transfer viewed in this light is in no sense a gift or subsidy from the citizens of the

stitutional. Arbitrarily differing amounts of federal expenditures per capita among states are not questioned.

more favored regions. It is no more a gift than that made from the citizens of the community property states to those of the non-community property states when income-splitting for tax purposes was extended over the whole nation to make the federal tax system more equitable. After the proposed inter-area transfer of funds, relatively greater fiscal pressure would be imposed upon citizens of the high income areas and relatively less upon those of the low income areas in comparison to those now imposed. But tradition gives little ground for continuing inequities, and we normally give short shrift to the individual who has continued to escape a share of his fiscal burden.

The policy implications of adopting the equity principle as a long-run goal for adjustment policy are far-reaching. Applied to the existing structure of intergovernmental fiscal relations in the United States, several steps are indicated. *First,* the elimination of the many matching provisions in the present grant-in-aid program is essential before progress can be made in any equalization policy. These provisions have served to prevent the whole grant-in-aid system from accomplishing any fiscal equalization between the rich and the poor areas at all.

A *second* and major implication is that the equity approach provides a justification for inter-area transfers independent of any particular public service or group of services. In the past, the principle of fiscal need has been combined with the principle of national interest with the result that grants have been justified only in specific service areas (highways, vocational education, etc.). There is, of course, legitimate justification for federal grants to states with the objective of furthering certain national interests, for example, minimum standards in educational services. But such grant-in-aid programs should be sharply divorced from the basic equalization policy. It seems highly probable that, if an equalization policy of the sort proposed here were carried out, national interests would be adequately served without any national government direction of state expenditure. The low income states provide deficient educational standards largely because of their fiscal plight; remove this, and it seems likely that their service standards would approach those of other states without any restraints upon state budgetary freedom. The acceptance of the equity objective, therefore, could lend support to a policy of broadening the functions for which grants are made, and of extending broadened conditional grants to other public service areas.

Ultimately, an essential step, if equalization is to be carried out *via* grants to states, and one which will not be easy to accomplish, is the entire elimination of directional conditions in federal grants to states and the substitution of unconditional grants. The equity principle provides an adequate justification for grants wholly unconditional, but traditional barriers against the unconditional intergovernmental transfer of funds, especially in the United States, are likely to loom large. The principle of financial responsibility which says, in effect, that "legislatures can be trusted to spend if required to tax accordingly,"[30] and not otherwise, is strong and has certain intrinsic merit when considered in isolation. But as is the case with the traditional principle of equity, the substitution of a federal political structure for a unitary one transforms the setting within which the principle may be applied. The fact that the central government must enter the adjustment process and transfer funds to effectuate equity in the over-all fiscal system does not therefore imply that the central government should be allowed to direct the recipient states in the allocation of their expenditure. There seems no apparent reason why there should be more central interference or direction in the financial operation of the recipient states than in that of the non-recipient states. States are made claimant through no fault of their own or of their respective citizens. They are made claimant by the income distribution arising from a resource allocation and payment in a national economy. Once it is recognized that the transfers are adjustments which are necessary to coordinate the federal political structure with a national economy, and as such are ethically due the citizens of the low income state units, then the freedom of these citizens to choose the pattern of their states' expenditure follows.

This concept of financial responsibility is, however, so strong that progress will perhaps require some compromise with it. Sub-

30. Henry C. Simons, "Hansen on Fiscal Policy," *Journal of Political Economy,* L (1942), 178.

stantial progress can be made in intergovernmental transfer policy by the gradual substitution of procedural for directional conditions. Movement in this direction can be made while observing the fiscal responsibility principle and still not greatly reducing the budgetary independence of the states.

However, as pointed out above, these problems which arise in any intergovernmental policy utilizing revenue transfers, disappear when the method of geographically discriminatory personal income taxation is adopted. No governmental unit receives revenue other than what is internally raised within its fiscal system; therefore, neither the principle of financial responsibility nor that of state fiscal independence is violated. This method of adjustment, however, can only be expected to become positive policy after there is a more widespread recognition of the basic elements of the fiscal problem of federalism, and the advantages of this method over others have been clearly impressed upon the public by competent authorities.

VI

The fiscal problem of federalism discussed here is not likely to become less acute. As the need for an ever-expanding scope of public services increases, with especial emphasis on the social services, the divergencies in fiscal capacities among state units will be more evidenced. The *laissez faire* result will be the ultimate centralization of a large share of effective political power, either directly through the assumption by the central government of traditional state and local functions, or indirectly through restraining financial conditions in an expanded grant-in-aid system. Therefore, those who desire to see maintained a truly decentralized political structure in the power sense, must take some action in support of proposals aimed at adjusting these interstate fiscal differences. Heretofore, little progress has been made, although increasing attention has been given to the problem. The failure to take positive steps may, in part, have been due to the lack of a specific long-run objective for policy. The equity principle presented here possibly offers an objective which, if accepted, can serve as the basis for the development of a rational intergovernmental fiscal adjustment system.

INDEX OF AUTHORS

Abbott, L., 126n, 138n
Adams, T. S., 48
Adarkar, B. P., 170n, 179n, 185
Allen, E. D., 16
Arrow, Kenneth, 5, 75, 92n, 93n, 94n, 102n
Asimakopulos, A., 80

Bailey, M. J., 154n, 168n, 169
Barna, Tibor, 16, 21
Barone, E., 24, 34, 36-37, 46, 65, 66n, 67-68, 73, 151-53, 167
Bastable, C. F., 15-16
Baumol, W. J., 77n, 94n, 113n
Benham, F. C., 25, 177n
Benson, G. C. S., 170n
Bergson, A., 107, 112, 117
Black, Duncan, 85n
Blum, Walter J., 45n
Borgatta, G., 35, 36n, 39n, 65, 68-72, 151
Bowen, H. R., 72n, 99n
Break, G. F., 151, 153, 154
Brown, H. G., 126, 140
Brownlee, O. H., 16

Carritt, E. F., 101n
Clark, Jane P., 170n
Cohen-Stuart, A. J., 45
Commons, J. R., 26
Conigliani, C., 65, 66
Cosciani, C., 36-37, 40, 65-68

Dahl, Robert A., 82n, 83n, 91n, 94n, 95n, 99n, 101n, 104n
Del Vecchio, G., 24, 39n, 71, 72
De Viti De Marco, A., 7, 13n, 14, 16, 24, 30, 31-35, 39-44, 50-59, 65, 68, 73
Downs, Anthony, 33n
Due, John, 126, 130-31, 148-49

Edgeworth, F. Y., 10, 45-46
Einaudi, Luigi, 24, 29n, 30n, 34, 36, 39, 41, 45-51, 65, 68, 73

Fasiani, Mauro, 36-37, 40, 50, 60, 64, 69, 70n, 74, 151
Ferrara, Francesco, 25, 27-31, 34, 38, 41, 71, 73
Fisher, Irving, 50
Friedman, Milton, 105, 143, 151-54, 161n, 167, 169
Fubini, R., 38, 71

Gangemi, L., 73
Gobbi, U., 47, 69n, 154n
Goodman, Leo, 80n
Graaff, J., 107
Graham, Frank D., 14n
Greenwood, Gordon, 173n
Griziotti, B., 26, 49, 56-57, 60n, 74

Haavelmo, T., 94n
Harriss, C. L., 19n
Hayek, F. A., 91n, 93n

Henderson, A. M., 93n
Hicks, J. R., 17, 107, 112
Hicks, U. K., 17
Hildreth, C., 80n

Jenkins, H. P. B., 126, 134-37, 146-48, 159n
Johnson, Byron L., 176n
Jones, William H., 178
Joseph, M. F. W., 69, 151

Kaizl, G., 16
Kaldor, N., 50n, 107, 112
Kalven, H., 45n
Kemp, Murray, 80n
Knight, F. H., 92, 100

Leland, S. E., 173n
Lindahl, Erik, 13n, 35
Lindblom, C. E., 82n, 83n, 91n, 94n, 95n, 99n, 101n, 104n
Little, I. M. D., 75n, 78n, 151, 154

Machlup, F., 128n
Maffezzoni, F., 57n, 58n
Markowitz, Harry, 80n
Marshall, Alfred, 70-71
Masci, G., 37, 39n
Maxwell, J. A., 170n
McQueen, R., 174n
Mill, J. S., 15, 45, 50, 175n
Mises, Ludwig von, 96, 98n
Montemartini, G., 24, 65-66
Mosca, G., 32
Murray, R. A., 36, 65-66
Musgrave, R. A., 20, 24n, 33n, 72n, 106n, 126, 131-34, 143, 146, 155

Neal, A. C., 95n
Nevins, R. A., 85n
Nichols, R. F., 173n

Pantaleoni, M., 13n, 24, 30-32, 39, 66, 73, 154
Papi, G., 44n
Pareto, V., 27, 32, 36, 65, 69-70, 73, 106, 112
Parravicini, G., 24, 125, 137, 148-49
Parsons, Talcott, 93n
Peacock, A. T., 24n, 33n, 106n
Philbrook, C., 98n
Phipps, C. G., 153
Pigou, A. C., 10, 30n, 44, 175n
Polanyi, Michael, 88, 101n
Puviani, A., 36-37, 59-64

Reynaud, P. L., 60n
Ricardo, David, 51-59
Ricca-Salerno, P., 37
Ricci, U., 47
Richenburg, L. J., 85n
Robbins, Lionel, 80
Rolph, Earl, 70n, 125-30, 144, 151, 154
Rothenberg, Jerome, 75n, 78n

Samuelson, P. A., 72n, 107, 112, 117
Sax, Emil, 13n, 31, 36
Say, J. B., 14
Schoeffler, S., 85
Schultz, W. J., 19n
Scitovsky, T., 107, 112
Seligman, E. R. A., 48
Sensini, G., 70n
Simons, Henry, 16, 25, 51n, 72, 126n, 188n
Spengler, J. J., 96
Steve, Sergio, 24
Stigler, George, 115
Stockfisch, J. A., 48

Tabatoni, P., 33n
Tun Thin, 20

Vinci, F., 60n

Wagner, Adolph, 13n
Walker, David, 151
Weber, Max, 93n
Weldon, J. C., 78n
Wicksell, Knut, 4-5, 15, 17n, 33, 35, 66, 68, 72-73, 84, 106n, 119

INDEX OF SUBJECTS

Ability-to-pay, principle of taxation, 47
Aggravative, fiscal system, 18
Alternatives, of voting and market, 96-98
Asymmetry, fiscal, 9
Austrian theory of capital, and tax incidence, 133

Balanced-budget approach, to tax incidence, 127
Benefit, principle of taxation, 12, 13
Brigandage, conception of tax, 39
Budgetary theory, and fiscal illusion, 63
Budgeting, pure theory of, 9
Burden, of extraordinary tax, 53; of public debt, 53; of tax, 144

Capitalization, of tax, 47-49
Centralization, in collective choice, 91
Certainty, in voting and market choices, 91-93
Ceteris paribus, in tax analysis, 142-43
Choice, collective, and free markets, 86-88; of individual, in voting and market, 90-104; and uncertainty, 92
Classical economics, influence on Italian fiscal tradition, 27
Classification, of fiscal systems, 18; of tax systems, 19
Coercion, and fiscal choice, 64-68; as function of state, 65-66
Collective choice, and majority decision, 82-86; and free markets, 86-88; centralized and decentralized, 91
Comparative tax analysis, 68-69; and methodology, 151-69
Comparisons, of tax burdens, 17
Compensation, principle, 107, 162; and status quo, 111-12; in welfare economics, 111-13; in tax analysis, 168
Conditional grants-in-aid, 188
Consensus, and majority rule, 83, 119-22; as test of hypotheses, 110; among reasonable men, 118-19
Consistency, in collective choice, 81; of choice, and market mechanism, 87
Constitutional requirements, for tax uniformity, 185
Consumers' surplus, 13, 69, 155
Cooperative conception of state, 34
Cost-push inflation, 149
Criterion of efficiency, 108
Debt, theory, Italian contribution, 51-59; burden of, 53; repayment, 58-59

Decentralization, in political structure and national economy, 172
Demand curve, Marshallian, 143; Friedman-Bailey type, 169; Hicksian type, 169

Demand elasticity, of public services, 44
Direct taxation, compared with indirect, 151-69
Discrimination, in taxation among regions, 184
Double taxation, of savings, 49-51

Economic integration, national, 172
Economists, as scientists, 105
Edgeworth, tax principle, 10
Efficiency, Pareto sense, 106; and omniscience, 107-11
"Einkommen," conception of income, 51
Elasticity of demand, for public services, 44
Equalitarian, fiscal systems, 18
Equality, of power, 100
Equalization, fiscal, among states, 174
Equal treatment, for equals, and federalism, 174-76
Equal yield, of taxes compared, 158-59
Equi-marginal sacrifice, principle of taxation, 10
Equity, fiscal, and federalism, 170-89; principle, 170-89; limitations to tax side, 176
Equivalence, between taxes and loans, Ricardian thesis, 51-59
"Ertrag," conception of income, 51
Ethical neutrality, and political economy, 109
Ethical precepts, and interstate equality, 174
Excess benefits, of excise tax, 165-66
Excess burden, controversy, 6; of excise tax, 151-69; and methodology, 152
Expenditure tax, 50
Expenditure variables, 10
Externalities, 113-14
Extraordinary taxes, and loans, 51-59

Federalism, and fiscal equity, 170-89
Financial authority, defined, 170; in federalism, 170
Fiscal brain, 10
Fiscal capacity, and federalism, 173-74; interstate differences, 174
Fiscal equity, and federalism, 170-89
Fiscal equalization, interstate, 174
Fiscal illusion, 59-64
Fiscal marginalism, 9
Fiscal neutrality, in geographic sense, 178
Fiscal pressures, in federalism, 178
Fiscal residuum, 17, 176-80
Fiscal responsibility, 188
Fiscal scientist, 21
Fiscal systems, classification, 18
Flint v. Stone Tracy Co., 185
Foundations, political, for pure theory of government finance, 8
Freedom, distinguished from power, 100
Free markets, and collective choices, 86-88
Functional finance, 12

General equilibrium, theory of, 32
General possibility theorem, Arrow's, 77
General welfare, 9, 12; Pareto criteria for, 67
Geographical location, and equity principle, 175-76
Giffen's paradox, 169
Gift taxation, and fiscal illusion, 61
Government finance, pure theory of, 8-23
Grants-in-aid, 187-88

Head Money Cases, 185
Hicksian demand curve, 169

Ideal output, 108
Ideal tax system, of De Viti De Marco, 42
Illusion, fiscal, 59-64
"Imposta-grandine," conception of tax, 39-40; and tax capitalization, 48

Incidence, and fiscal illusion, 62; theory and methodology, 125-50; true and false, 146-48; of tax and monetary assumptions, 148
Income effect, of tax, 128
Income redistribution, and federal system, 179
Income tax, and consumption tax, 68-69
Income taxation, and regional discrimination, 184
Indifference curves, applied to tax problems, 68
Indirect taxation, and fiscal illusion, 61; compared with direct taxation, 151-69
Individual choice, in voting and market, 90-104
Individualistic theory of state, 6, 11-22, 35
Indivisibility, and market choice, 99
Inflation, and fiscal illusion, 61; cost-push, 149
Interdependence, among tax and expenditure variables, 10; in fiscal account, 22; of economy, 168
Intergovernmental fiscal problems, 170-89
Interstate differences, in fiscal capacity, 174

Keynesian revolution, effects on debt theory, 57
Knowledge of alternatives, in voting and market choice, 91
Knowlton vs Moore, 185

Law, and political economy, 115
Least aggregate sacrifice, principle of taxation, 10
Loans, and taxes compared, 51-59
Lump-sum taxation, 44, 154

Majority decision, and collective choice, 82-86
Majority rule, as a welfare function, 77; and consensus, 83, 119-22
Majority tyranny, 84
Marginalism, fiscal, 9
Marginal productivity theory, applied to fiscal problem, 43
Marginal utility, theory of, 31
Market, as a welfare function, 77
Market choice, compared with voting, 90-104
Market mechanism, and consistency of choice, 87
Marshallian consumers' surplus, 13
Marshallian demand curve, 143
Marshallian influence, on fiscal theory, 70
Marshallian partial equilibrium, 6, 32
Marxist conception of class, 32
Matching grants-in-aid, 187-88
Methodology, of Italian fiscal theory, 38-41; of incidence theory, 125-50; and comparative tax analysis, 151-69
Minimum sacrifice, theory of taxation, 45-47
Minority, and market choices, 98
Monetary framework, for tax analysis, 147-49
Monopoly, conception of state, 34

National economy, and fiscal problem of federalism, 177-78
Neighborhood effects, 113-14
Neutrality, fiscal, 178
Neutral money, 150
Neutral tax system, 44-45

Old tax, and fiscal illusion, 62
Omniscience, and efficiency and welfare economics, 107-11
One-dollar-one-vote analogy, 90-104
Optimality, in Pareto sense, 106; Paretian, and excise tax, 153
Optimal tax, 45
Optimum allocation of public expenditures, 9
Optimum collective choices, 88
Optimum values for tax variables, 10
Organic conception of state, 8-11, 37, 79

Paradox of voting, 82-83
Paretian conditions for optimality, 106
Paretian criteria, for welfare, 67, 106; for optimality and tax, 153, 161
Pareto rule, 106-12
Partial equilibrium analysis, Marshallian, 32; methodology, 126; Friedman's usage, 167
Participation, in social decisions, 93-95
Pigovian tax principle, 10
Political economy, and positive economics, 105-24; and ethical neutrality, 109; and changes in law, 113
Political equality, 100
Political foundations, for pure theory of government finance, 8
Poll taxation, 14
Positive economics, and welfare economics, 105-24
Power, in voting and market choices, 100
Presumptive efficiency, 108-11
Price-allocation, effects of tax, 128
Production possibility, model for comparative tax analysis, 152
Productivity, of public services, 41-45
Progressive taxation, 19, 45
Proportional taxation, and redistribution, 19; De Viti De Marco argument, 42
Public debt, burden of, 53; repayment, 58-59
Public domain, and fiscal illusion, 61
Public expenditures, optimum allocation of, 9; Pantaleoni's theory, 31
Public services, as consumption, 41; as inputs and productive factors, 41-45; and elasticity of demand, 44
Pure democracy, one form of decision-making, 91

Quid pro quo, between individual and government, 12-13, 19; premise, 17; principle of taxation, 172

Rationality, social, 78-81; in market and voting choices, 101
Redistribution, and fiscal system, 18; and federal system, 179
Regressive taxation, for system, 19; and redistribution, 20
Relative unanimity, 119
Repayment, of public debt, 58-59
Representative man, as characteristic of group, 169
Residuum, fiscal, 17, 170-80
Responsibility, in social choice, 95-96; fiscal, 188
Ricardian-Marshallian tradition, in fiscal thought, 38
Ricardian public debt theory, 51-59
Ricardian rent theory, 28
Ruling class, theory of, 32-33; and fiscal choice, 65; conception of fiscal process, 68

Sacrifice, principle of taxation, 10, 45-47
Savings, double taxation of, 49-51
Scientific approach to fiscal theory, 33-34
Single-peaked orderings, 77
Single tax, 30
Social choice, 75-79, 95-96
Social decision-making, participation in, 93-95
Social rationality, 78-81
Social utility, 9, 175
Social welfare function, 68, 76-78, 107, 117-18
Spontaneous order, and market economy, 88
Status quo fiscal systems, 18
Surplus, consumers', 13, 69

Tax, considered as price, 40
Taxation, compared with loans, 51-59; indirect of gifts, and fiscal illusion, 61; geographical discrimination in, 184

Tax burden comparisons, 17
Tax capitalization, 47-49
Tax shifting, theory of, 32
Tax systems, classification, 19
Tax variables, 10
Transitivity, in social welfare function, 83
Tyranny, of majority, 84

Unanimity, principle of taxation, 66; Wicksell principle of, 68; and collective choice, 86; among reasonable men, 119; as test for hypotheses, 123
Uncertainty, of incidence, and fiscal illusion, 62; in voting and market, 92
Unconditional grants-in-aid, 188-89
Uniformity, of taxation, and intergovernmental transfers, 185
Utilitarians, and individualism, 80
Utility, social, 9, 11, 67, 175; theory of, 30-32; interpersonal comparability of, 46; Paretian maximum, 67; as subjectively quantifiable, 108

Voting, and public interest, 102
Voting choice, compared with market, 90-104
Voting paradox, 82-83

Wage-push inflation, 149
Walrasian models, 6, 39, 70
Welfare economics, 5, 71; and positive economics, 105-24; new, 106-07